Mark Oakley is Chancellor of St Paul's Cathedral. He is a writer, broadcaster and visiting lecturer in the Department of Theology and Religious Studies, King's College, London. He is the author of *The Collage of God* (Canterbury Press, 2001, reissued 2012) and *The Splash of Words: Believing in poetry* (Canterbury Press, 2016), and the compiler of *Readings for Weddings* (2004, reissued 2013) and *Readings for Funerals* (2015), both published by SPCK.

A GOOD YEAR

Edited by
Mark Oakley

First published in Great Britain in 2016

Society for Promoting Christian Knowledge
36 Causton Street
London SW1P 4ST
www.spck.org.uk

The author and publisher have made every effort to ensure that the external website and email addresses included in this book are correct and up to date at the time of going to press. The author and publisher are not responsible for the content, quality or continuing accessibility of the sites.

For copyright acknowledgements, see p. 121

British Library Cataloguing-in-Publication Data
A catalogue record for this book is available from the British Library

ISBN 978–0–281–07703–8
eBook ISBN 978–0–281–07704–5

Typeset by Graphicraft Limited, Hong Kong
First printed in Great Britain by Ashford Colour Press
Subsequently digitally printed in Great Britain

eBook by Graphicraft Limited, Hong Kong

Produced on paper from sustainable forests

For my colleagues
Simon Carter, Elizabeth Foy,
Donna McDowell and Barbara Ridpath,
who help to make the year good.

Contents

Introduction

―――――・●・●・――――――

Mark Oakley

In the Church of England's service of the ordination and consecration of a bishop, it states that bishops 'are to feed God's pilgrim people, and so build up the Body of Christ'.[1] At a time of discernible spiritual hunger, both inside and outside the Church, one of the ways in which that feeding can be done is by enabling and encouraging the Christian community to learn. In their ministry, bishops are asked to secure the integrity of the Church, which means making certain the gospel is explored for all its mysterious richness, and to ensure the scrutiny of ourselves and society. It also involves mining the Christian tradition for inspiration and, at the same time, making sure the questions of the contemporary world are addressed with honesty and openness. Christians learn not necessarily because they like information but because they desire formation: a forming of themselves into a better likeness of their Lord, out of gratitude to the one who made them. What they discover in the gospel, and the ways it has inspired and changed people before them, begins to translate into the ways they speak, listen and relate in their own day. It starts to shape priorities and to distil what matters. For the Christian, to learn is to deepen communion with the Origin of life and with those with whom we share that life. As St Benedict taught, a Christian community is a little school where we learn to relate to God, each other and ourselves. Learning is communion.

Because of their calling to feed the Christian Church and to secure its integrity, the St Paul's Cathedral Adult Learning Department invited bishops to come to teach some Christians and other exploring people about the way the Church divides the year into seasons. These seasons take shape so that faith can breathe in the poetic beauty of Christian belief through all the ways available to us: Scripture and preaching, hymns and songs, movement and colour, drama and debate, prayer and stillness. Because the passing into a new season of the Church's year can sometimes make its greatest impact in a place only by the changing of the altar frontal, we asked the bishops to tell us what they believed would make a 'good' observation of each season. How would a good Lent be spent? How can we journey through Holy Week fruitfully? How might we celebrate Easter well? What would a Christian Christmas look like? Four bishops came and delivered thoughtful talks that prompted a lot of honest and practical questions from the audience. You can view these events on the St Paul's website at <www.stpauls.co.uk/learning-faith/adult-learning/videos-podcasts>. Although Christians live the mysteries of the Christian faith simultaneously, the Church's tradition lays them out in a linear fashion and asks us to observe the particularity of those mysteries through a 12-month cycle. It became very clear during the conversations at St Paul's that this would be a tradition lost at great cost.

The Church of England had not yet ordained women bishops when we held the talks under the dome of the cathedral. When some asked whether we planned to publish the talks, we decided that we would but only alongside reflections on other seasons of the Church's year by women bishops – once they had arrived! In 2015, the first woman to be ordained and consecrated into the episcopate was Bishop Libby Lane, and we are thrilled that she agreed to write for this collection.

The tone and style of the contributions are inevitably varied. Some were originally written to be heard, some to be read. Some took shape 'on stage' with an audience; others were written in a quiet study. The bishops come from different traditions within the Church of England, so varied theological emphases occur. What unites them all is a deep passion for the seasons of the Church's year to be celebrated imaginatively and faithfully for the feeding of God's pilgrim people and the building up of the body of Christ.

Sarah Mullally begins this book by focusing us on the season of Advent. In the Roman Empire, when an emperor came to power and ceremonially entered a province or city, it was described as his 'advent' (Latin *adventus*: 'arrival'). A gold medallion found at Arras shows such an 'advent' in AD 296 of Constantius Chlorus at the gates of the City of London. Latin-speaking Christians borrowed the word and concept for Jesus Christ, their only Lord and Emperor, and invested it with the meaning of their Saviour's arrival. The second-century Christian apologist Justin Martyr wrote, 'it was foretold that there would be two advents of Christ: one in which he will appear in suffering and without honour and beauty; the second in which he will return in glory to judge all people'.[2] Over the centuries, Advent developed this dual significance, commemorating incarnation and preparing ourselves for the liberation of judgement, when we are seen at last, and recognized, for who we really are.

Advent is a season in the vocative. The great 'O's, when we call out to God to come to touch us back into a life worthy of the name, longingly give heart to the season. It is as if we say: 'Come to us and tell us who we have become, so we can admit it and then begin to change – but with your help.' Human bodies are quite good at healing themselves over time; a cut will mend quickly. Human souls are not so adept; they have to be healed from the outside, by being loved and believed in. Advent is the season when we are honest about our incompleteness and the need to be 'saved' by a love beyond ourselves. It is the time when we acknowledge that, for Christians, everything is as yet unfinished and that we will be inspirited by hope and the ability to wait. It is a season pregnant with God. The imagery and words of Advent poetically and riotously work hard to do some justice to our trust in that God who comes to us as we are and as we shall be. God loves us just as we are now and comes in incarnation to reveal this love. However, God loves us so much that he doesn't want us to remain the same; he comes to liberate us from the prisons and limitations of cold, closed hearts, preparing us for a share in his glory.

In Normandy, there used to be a tradition on Advent Sunday of paying children to run around the fields to bash haystacks so that all the rats came out of the harvest. It was a good day to do it. Our rats need dealing with if there is to be bread on the table. Advent is not for beginners. It exposes our darkness and the faults that are usually more forgivable than the ways in which we try to hide them.

Advent tells us to grow up, to face our facts, to cry out for a hand of healing and to be infused with a new story, a new script, a fresh way of seeing everything that might drop down into us and water our parched humanity. We need saving from ourselves and we need to prepare the straw for a birth within us. Advent dares us to stand looking towards heaven and praying out loud: 'We're ready; it's time to wake up. OK. Here goes – let redemption draw near.'

Rowan Williams typically explores Christmas with imagination and insights that feel both new to, and yet somehow at home in, the soul. Beginning with a look at some of the carols we sing at this time of year, he reminds us that difficulty is usually more important than quick clarity, and that the hard lines and incomprehensible images of some of our carols might be more important than we first imagine. He shows us that, although we call on God in Advent, we can never lure him down by being polite or behaving well. God can't help but overflow into a world of his making. Trying to convince God to like us would be as futile as trying to convince a waterfall to be wet.

As I read his reflection, I found myself thinking of those other carols found in the composer Benjamin Britten's *Ceremony of Carols*. Britten wrote this work while on a cramped, airless cargo vessel, travelling from the USA to England in 1942. Not only did Britten have to battle against the crew's swearing and constant whistling but he was also sailing at the height of the U-boat attacks in the Atlantic. The relaxed joyfulness of the music contrasts somewhat with what was a dangerous and precarious journey.

While stopping in Nova Scotia, Britten picked up a book of medieval poems, from which some of the texts for his

Ceremony of Carols came. Britten, as usual, took words that didn't at first appear to be made for song and allowed his music to be true to the language, keeping its lifeblood and earthiness. His choral piece is in 11 movements and is sung in the context of processional and recessional chanting. It is as if the story it celebrates is brought into our midst and then taken beyond our reach, reflecting the Christian desire for the story of Christ to be within us, coupled with the sense that it feels distant, eternal, beyond us. We sense innocence before its loss, a cycle of arrival and departure, reverence and rebellion, devotion and dereliction. We are faced with the fragile, temperamental, imperfect people God comes to and the eternal heart from which Christ comes. In one poem, simple Latin phrases hold the form together and, for me, sum up the celebration of Christmas: *res miranda, pares forma, gaudeamus, transeamus* – marvellous thing, of equal form, let us rejoice, let us cross over and follow.

Libby Lane then takes us on the Epiphany journey. Epiphany has grabbed the human imagination with great force. Not only are the hymns we sing some of the very best we have, the art and poetry depicting the Magi some of the most striking, but also the traditions of Epiphany are great fun – from Epiphany cakes to the blessing of orchards, from the Italian *La Befana* to the blessing of boats. Epiphany in the West first focuses on the Magi but then dives into the baptismal waters of the Jordan when Jesus meets his cousin John. Then it draws us into the first miracle of John's Gospel, the transformation of water into wine. Bishop Libby reminds us that the Feast of St Paul also falls within the season of Epiphany. It seems more than appropriate that the great apostle to the Gentiles is reverenced in this season, when the gospel's generosity and reach is the pulse of our prayer.

At first, of course, the Magi were thought of as astrologers (hence their concern with the stars) and were said to have come in droves, not just three (nowhere does it say there were three in the Gospels); they stabilized (excuse the pun) at three, no doubt because there were three gifts – one each. No one before Tertullian in the second century ever thought of the wise men as kings. In the wall paintings of the catacombs and in some Byzantine mosaics, the Magi wore Mithraic robes. No one actually named them Balthazar, Melchior and Caspar until the ninth century. These names have led to that other Epiphany tradition of marking our doorways with chalk: writing the year and the initials of the Magi – CMB – which can also stand for *Christus mansionem benedicat*: 'Christ bless this home'. In Syria, though, the Magi are known as Larvandad, Harmisdas and Gushnasaph. The Venerable Bede suggested they represented the entire world – one came from Asia, one from Africa and one from Europe – and so one, from the fifteenth century onwards, is often depicted as being black. If you go to the Cathedral at Autun, you'll see a stone sculpture of the three kings tucked up in bed together (I'm not sure how well this sits with the Bishops' Guidelines!). They are under a large blanket all wearing their crowns like night caps. An angel wakes them and points to the star. One of them has his eyes wide open, one is bleary-eyed and the third is sound asleep. These are the three spiritual states of humanity.

In the fourth century, it was Prudentius who began the business of giving different mystic meanings to the gifts. You find these in our carols: 'Incense doth their God disclose, gold the King of kings proclaimeth, myrrh his sepulchre foreshows'.[3] Of course, if they were astrologers and showmen, glittering gold and screens of smoke were probably part of their show. To lay those props aside, in front of Christ, then, is more than giving posh presents; it is laying down a livelihood – even a life – built on falsity for the sake of a more human way.

By taking us to the Jordan, Epiphany also helps us to recall the baptism of Jesus and our consequent baptism. All the noise of the shoreline, all the world's harsh and destructive messaging and jaundiced takes on life, is, for one under-water moment, drowned out; the only thing you can hear is your own heart beating. You then emerge, take a gulp of fresh air and listen to the only words that matter – not from the crowd but from heaven: 'You are my beloved child.' Our calling is to live up to these words and not to live down to what the world can tell us about ourselves. This is where we discover our human dignity, rooted in the message of heaven as the water laps over us. As do the Magi, we return home by another road. Our water turns into the intoxicating wine of love towards us and in its jars it overflows enough for us to share it with everyone else. Epiphany is a feast time for celebrating Christian identity and partnership.

Justin Welby takes us into the desert and argues for a less individualistic approach to Lent. The day before Lent begins, many of us tuck in to pancakes – a pancake is a helpful visual aid for what Lent is trying to confront. Pancakes are fat and flat. They are like our modern souls. Lent is an invitation to a spiritual adventure of confronting head on the fat and the flat in us. It scrutinizes how we live our lives, how we have become consumers instead of citizens, how we can buy and eat more and more because of other hungers that lie deep down. Lent asks if we are a society with lots to live *with* but little sense of what to live *for*. What is it that we really want when we pick up yet another gadget, shirt, book or sandwich?

Lent is not the 'thou shalt not' season but a refreshing snowfall in the soul that asks us gently, without apology, whether our lives are in some sort of balance. It is a time of fasting, of learning what we can live without to bring better proportion to living and relating. It asks us to attend to our needs, not our wants. It asks us to fast, not just from coffee but also from the angry word, the quick judgement, the indifferent credit card. We all need to fast somewhere.

A flat life is one where we kill time before time kills us. Lent throws a lifebelt to us and, in a season of Christian schooling as I mentioned above, calls us back to learn how to relate to God, each other and ourselves. It is a season that places the compass back in the hand to make sure we don't hate our neighbours as ourselves but are loving them as ourselves. It is the season that reiterates U-turns can be good. As we receive ash marks on Ash Wednesday, the first stroke makes an 'I' and then the second crosses it and makes it into the sign of Christ. The sign is made on the (fore)head, that protective case for the brain, the seat of the will. Fragile and bruised by the past, that brain is gently caressed with the ash of mortality in a symbol of eternity. 'Be faithful to Christ', we are told, 'as he is faithful to you.' Self-justification is exhausting and pointless. It has been said that living gracefully is giving more than you owe and receiving more than you deserve. The stark beauty of Lent confirms both insights to be true.

A few years ago, I saw Jacob Epstein's statue of Adam. Made in 1938, it is towering, majestic, full of potential, energy

and life. It is also very noticeably naked. The sculpture has
a tragic history. Within 20 years, it ended up in a New York
peepshow and a Blackpool basement waxwork museum,
debased for naughty titters, a few ready bucks, and locked in
the dark. Epstein was heartbroken. Adam, of course, means
'humankind' and the history of Epstein's work outlines what
we have done to those other beautiful works of art called
us. Lent says enough is enough. It's well past time to make
amendments. No more can we be, in T. S. Eliot's words,
'Distracted from distraction by distraction'.[4]

Stephen Cottrell, in his usual firefly style of peppering us
with light when things appear gloomy, leads us through the
pivotal days of Holy Week. He tells us to celebrate the days
with gusto: 'If you've got it flaunt it!' For St John Chrysostom,
the last seven days of Christ's redeeming work on earth con-
stituted the Great Week because 'great things were wrought
at this time by the Lord'.[5] The full drama of our salvation
is to be found in the days of Holy Week and we are negligent
if we prefer some sort of 'Triduum-lite' faith. By praying
through Holy Week, you open up the possibility that you
might yet be converted by love rather than fear.

Palm Sunday sees Pontius Pilate entering Jerusalem to make
sure all possible riots are controlled during the Passover. He
comes into the city with his cavalry and all the imperial pomp
and plumage. On the other side of the city, a man comes
into the same city on a donkey. Later in the story, each man
will hold a bowl of water. The Roman washes his hands of
all responsibility; the Jewish teacher uses the water to wash
his followers' feet. In the upper room of Maundy Thursday,
we learn what Marilynne Robinson notes in her novel *Gilead*:
'Love is holy because it is like grace – the worthiness of its

object is never really what matters.'⁶ Pontius Pilate is clearly concerned about what his superiors will make of his management. Jesus asks that he be remembered in the sharing of bread, the passing round of a cup and by his followers' loving one another.

In the later despair of Calvary, it appears that the power of Rome and its compromised partners have won the day, and that God seems to have forsaken the man hanging on a cross. His followers, however, come to see that, although God seemed to have been absent on that tragic afternoon, he had actually never been closer to his creation. The life of courageous love that is executed for its rebellion and outspoken solidarity with the marginalized, the disciples come to understand, was the purest reflection of God's eternal outpouring of love towards his own people, ever seeking to be close, to heal and make whole.

To travel through the intense, dramatic liturgies of Holy Week is both to remember Christ and his love and to re-member him – to put him together as his body now on earth – translating the hours of that week into the days and years of our lives. You can read the Scriptures and study the thoughts of many a theologian to see how the world was redeemed. But reading alone will never affect you in the same way as being part of a dramatic enactment of those holy days of our Christian faith; God is not the object of our knowledge but the cause of our wonder.

Stephen Conway, through visual art, explores the celebration of Eastertide – a celebration that never ends for the Christian community as it is the season that is always present. One way that Eastern Christians have invited us to develop eyes of faith is through those windows on to eternity we call icons. Typically, most icons of the resurrection depict Jesus standing on a precarious-looking bridge. He stands in the middle; beneath his feet are shattered gates, broken chains and padlocks scattered about. Down in a dark cave you see an ancient Adam and Eve; Jesus is offering his hands to them and is lifting them out of the hole they are both in, out of their hell. This is resurrection as liberation, liberation into a new heaven and a new earth. In some icons, it looks as if Jesus is not only pulling Adam and Eve up but also towards each other. One of the first things Adam does after the fall is blame Eve; Eve then blames the snake. It is as if Jesus both liberates them and reintroduces them after their blaming match. He dissolves loneliness by showing us how we are compulsive dividers, compulsive grumblers, and by offering us a bridge back to life. Here, resurrection is not just a moment of seeing the faithfulness of God's love, which searches us out and won't give up on us, but it's also a moment when human beings are reintroduced to one another across the gulfs they have constructed. This is resurrection as defrosting. It is resurrection as a second look at one another – a second look, not a first impression.

One of the ways Easter has been celebrated through the generations is by the gift of laughter. Although it's said that German humour is no laughing matter, it was in parts of Bavaria where *risus paschalis*, the laughter of Easter, was celebrated. Christians were actively encouraged to laugh in church because laughter was the only true way to celebrate resurrection – after all, Jesus had played a joke on death. The preacher would tell jokes to try to start the congregation off. Those who remember Larry Grayson will recall that he used to begin his stage act by coming on and telling us that he didn't feel well. In fact, he said, 'I feel as limp as a vicar's handshake.' Well, clergy jokes, as we painfully know, can be just as limp, but it seems a medieval Easter often saw the priest telling unsophisticated gags that were also often obscene. Undoubtedly, not all local bishops approved.

Communities would also continue the merriment at Eastertide. In England, for instance, we can find activities such as Pace-Egging, Holly Bussing, Coal Carrying and Bottle Kicking. In the past, if you went to watch a medieval Mystery Play, you would have seen a lot of bawdy characters and a great deal of riotous fun as the joy of the history of our salvation was performed. When churches were built, there was often a lot of playfulness going on in the architecture and decoration. Diarmaid MacCulloch's marvellous book on the Reformation[7] reminds us of the little country church in Preston Bissett where, as the priest celebrated mass, he would have looked at a very cheeky pair of buttocks carved under the entrance to the chancel, where a man had been carved bent over, holding up the arch, its weight on his shoulders. So the priest, as he celebrated Christ's redemption of the human body, as well as the soul, was made to look at the medieval equivalent of a builder's bum. Higher up, equally naughty and provocative things were often sculpted as gargoyles. So, what was going on in those past times, before the Puritans and Roundheads got to work on us all? MacCulloch is clear: 'This was a religion where shouts of laughter as well as roars of rage were common in church',[8] where the clergy, at most, waged a very half-hearted battle against fun.

Our forebears knew that laughter is a promise of redemption and faith is trust in the promise being kept. Laughter levels and draws people together; it reveals our foibles and limits, keeps pomposity at bay and hints at something transcendent.

whose language is that of longing for us, the sound that wakes us up, rallies us. A reminder too that God *speaks*, not merely *spake*.

In England, where Pentecost was known as Whitsun because of the white clothes that people baptized on the day wore, there were Whitsun ales to drink (in honour of those Spirit-filled disciples people thought were tipsy). Horse racing was the sport of the day, commemorating the galloping Spirit, carrying us on, journeying with us on our race through time. In the Oriental churches, congregations had services of genuflexion (knee bending) and poetry, to signify the Spirit making us bend to his will, showing us what it is like to live as natives, not as tourists, in the kingdom of God. Poetry and imagination – the only human ways to describe such an indescribable mystery that is both strange and yet home. Theology, as poetry, would make no sense if read quickly or with a noisy background.

In Russia, flowers and supple green branches are carried to church – because the Spirit is forever fresh and, like buds pregnant with potential, coming to his fullest blossom in the human heart. St Paul told us how the Spirit flowers in us: love, joy, peace, patience, kindness, goodness, faithfulness, gentleness, self-control. And, talking of flowers, in Italy, it was the custom to scatter rose petals from the ceiling of the churches to recall the little red fiery tongues over the disciples' heads, so Whitsun in Italy is called *Pascha rosatum*. The nearest we come to this in the UK is the wearing of red vestments, a sign that we are to be clothed with the Spirit, to catch fire. As we say together in the Creed: 'I believe in the Holy Spirit, the Lord, the giver of Life' – not 'existence' but 'life'.

It would be tempting to think that Pentecost rounds off the seasons of the Christian year but, in fact, it begins that great period known strangely as 'ordinary time'. Most churches go back to using green vestments over these weeks, suggesting a time of fertile growth for deepening our understanding of, and fruitfulness in, the mysteries that have been celebrated since Advent. This deepening can only be done in the hope of Easter and the joy of God's Spirit. This is presumably why at Salisbury, instead of green, the cathedral continues the ancient Sarum tradition of continuing to use red, as all ordinary time for a Christian is fired by God's creative and reconciling Spirit. Red is the colour of fire: at once both a symbol of God's presence and warmth and also of God's scorching truth that burns away dross and unreality. It sounds frightening but liberating – and that's what it means to be an ordinary Christian.

At the Edinburgh Festival in 2000, there was a memorable production of Shakespeare's *The Tempest*, directed by Chris Goode. The play begins with a storm and a shipwreck and takes us to an island – often in literature and myth a place of human testing, a place of magical but dangerous dislocation of the soul. The production in Edinburgh was performed in local people's houses and flats. You offered your home and the six actors turned up like strolling players and began the play without any preliminary fuss. It took place in semi-darkness with improvised lighting from torches, bicycle lamps, candles and fairy lights. At the end, the actors evaporated into the night, like shy spirits, without even taking a bow. It was a stark reminder that theatre is an experience you have, not a place you go to.

Chris Goode believed a home was simply the best place to put on a play that is all about changing perceptions, altered states and geographical confusions. Performing in people's homes allowed him and the cast to take the audience on a journey in which the familiar became disconcertingly unfamiliar. So, in an Edinburgh flat, a bedroom doorway became Caliban's lair and, in a kitchen, Ferdinand was found undertaking Prospero's tasks, better known as 'washing-up'. Miranda and Prospero's murmured conversation, heard just a foot away, was Shakespeare spoken in your living room, not declaimed on a stage; it was as if you were eavesdropping. When the play finished, in pitch darkness, after being stunned for a few seconds, the audience came to, as if they were waking from a dream, to find the actors gone. And, at every performance, somewhere in the home, the actors had left behind a small paper boat, on the mantelpiece or by the bed or resting by the window. A small reminder that it hadn't all been a dream; it had happened under your own roof.

Early Christians spoke of Jesus as Word, walking into the land of our homes, visiting us for a short time and, in that time, subverting us, our priorities and selfish comforts, our so-called 'common' sense and our deep and destructive prejudices. He was making the familiar strange again. In that short span, he was re-picturing God for us, redefining the boundaries of love, if there are such things. This man walks in and creates a storm of the human spirit, blasting complacency where it has become oppressive to you or others and creating a calm where struggling lives need assurance and peace. In many ways, before his coming, this life in our earth-home was a tempest of changing perceptions, altered states and talk of a kingdom far off that feels homely. He brought an energy, a hope, a new way of being that thawed the heart: 'If only you had the ears to hear,' he said. 'If only you could tune in your lives to this brave new world of God.'

A good Advent

Sarah Mullally
BISHOP OF CREDITON

The Advent wind begins to stir
With sea-like sounds in our Scotch fir;
It's dark at breakfast, dark at tea,
And in between we only see
Clouds hurrying across the sky
And rain-wet roads the wind blows dry
And branches bending to the gale
Against the skies all silver-pale.[1]

John Betjeman describes with great skill the mood of
December in Britain. Shadows gathering, wind and rain
demanding houses be warmed and curtains be drawn.

A season of deep shadows

Advent is a time of deep and dark shadows. The sun is
becoming increasingly short-lived in our sky, and when
the storm clouds come with one weather system on top of
another we wonder if it is ever going to shine again. This is
the season when light is scarce and shadows and darkness
reign. We recognize their presence and come face to face
with them throughout our world and in our personal lives
too. The shadows of the world – terrorism, political uncertainty and financial challenge – and the shadows of our

personal lives – shadows of death or illness, unemployment or broken relationships.

Into these shadows Betjeman's poem proclaims:

> The Advent bells call out 'Prepare,
> Your world is journeying to the birth
> Of God made Man for us on earth.'

The Advent voice calls to us across the centuries through Scripture. It is the call of God, a call of salvation and a call of hope.

Jesus belonged to a world where theology and politics went hand in hand. The Jews believed that God was the only God, and that they were God's chosen people. They lived with the promises of forgiveness articulated by Isaiah, Jeremiah and Ezekiel speaking of liberation, salvation and hope. It was into this world, on tiptoe with expectation, that we waited for Jesus to begin announcing that Israel's God was now at last becoming king to bring salvation and hope to all people.

> How beautiful upon the mountains
>   are the feet of the messenger who announces peace,
> who brings good news,
>   who announces salvation,
>   who says to Zion, 'Your God reigns.'
> Listen! Your sentinels lift up their voices,
>   together they sing for joy;
> for in plain sight they see
>   the return of the Lord to Zion.

Break forth together into singing,
  you ruins of Jerusalem;
for the Lord has comforted his people,
  he has redeemed Jerusalem.
The Lord has bared his holy arm
  before the eyes of all the nations;
and all the ends of the earth shall see
  the salvation of our God.

Depart, depart, go out from there!
  Touch no unclean thing;
go out from the midst of it, purify yourselves,
  you who carry the vessels of the Lord.
For you shall not go out in haste,
  and you shall not go in flight;
for the Lord will go before you,
  and the God of Israel will be your rearguard.

(Isaiah 52.7–12)

And from across Scripture and time the Advent bells call out about our salvation and hope; it is a call that brings light into the shadows: 'The people who walked in darkness have seen a great light; those who lived in a land of deep darkness' (Isaiah 9.2). It is a call that sees justice restored:

For a child has been born for us . . .
  and there shall be endless peace
for the throne of David and his kingdom.
  He will establish and uphold it
with justice and with righteousness
  from this time onwards and for evermore.

(Isaiah 9.6–7)

It is a call of peace and of hope. It is a call which proclaims that we have the right to be called children of God. It is a call of salvation which is not just to be celebrated – it is a call to be proclaimed. It is this hope which makes a good Advent.

As we enter Advent we risk being drawn into sentimentality – finding ourselves looking to our 'traditions', as if they provide us with our central heating, and closing our curtains on the world – so that we can find that warm safe place. As we enter Advent we risk withdrawing from the world as if we are able to avoid our shadows and the shadows of the world. A good Advent rather recognizes the shadows and that the light has come into the world. A good Advent recognizes that the light is coming into the world again and again and that the darkness will not overcome it.

To prepare ourselves for a good Advent is to be ready with our lamps lit just like those who are waiting for their master's return from the wedding banquet (Luke 12.35–48).

A time of waiting

In the wake of the act of terrorism in Paris at the end of November 2015 I found myself outside the Civic Centre in Exeter walking towards the Cathedral along with members of the Muslim community and Christian community, with those of faith and of no faith, to stand in silence outside the Cathedral as an act of solidarity, of peace and of hope. As we walked, we journeyed through the Christmas market as it opened and we walked under the Christmas lights as they were turned on. It was clear that for everyone but the Church, Christmas had arrived. We don't like waiting – not even for Christmas. And although waiting is counter-cultural, the Church enters four weeks of waiting – the season of Advent with its candles, carols, liturgy and readings as the world has already found Christmas. A good Advent is to hold Advent in a Christmas world.

Advent tells us we must wait. Lifting us beyond the routine and the obvious, Advent invites us to watch, to expect the unexpected and to live in hope today.

The church fathers did not pick 25 December to celebrate the birth of Christ because they thought it was the actual day Mary gave birth, but because that was the time when the pre-Christian people were celebrating the new birth of the sun. Christians, believing Jesus to be the true light of the world, thought this would be a perfect time to celebrate his birth. Our ancestors had ways to woo the sun god back. They would halt their normal activity, bring a wheel from their cart into their home and decorate it with greenery and candles (the origins of our Advent wreath). Then they would wait and pray for the return of the great light. So strong was their faith that, year after year, they succeeded in wooing it back!

Throughout the Gospels Jesus prepares the disciples for shadows. He prepares them, trying to help them understand that life in this broken world is going to be difficult. But in offering us a picture of deep shadows he also offers a picture of hope – Jesus comes to us.

We wait, living in hope, not only because God became incarnate in the Christ child, nor simply because the Christ promises to come yet again. We live in hope because Christ's reign is among us now. He promises to become incarnate in you and me as we live by God's Spirit, as we bear God's Spirit, as we embrace our future as God's future, working for justice and seeking peace, not simply for ourselves, but for everyone.

Advent, like Lent, is a time of waiting. Both are seasons of preparation, but Lent and Advent are not the same. Lent is for self-examination, a stripping away of the layers with which we have covered ourselves, whatever they are, seeing the truth about ourselves. Advent is a time not to examine ourselves but to examine God, to look for God and his hope. So the season is full of the imagery of God breaking into the settled ways of the world, and it matters a lot less whether we know what is wrong with ourselves than that we know the hope of God.

At the start of Advent each year Salisbury Cathedral holds its 'From darkness into light' service over three evenings. Out of total darkness and silence, the much loved service builds to a climax with the 750-year-old building ablaze with more than 1,300 candles. The Cathedral's Advent services are a unique blend of theatre and worship, inspired by ancient liturgical and musical traditions. A candlelit procession of 32 cathedral choristers, accompanied by adult singers, wends its way around the medieval building, pausing among the congregation to sing. From the West Gallery high above the nave the sound of the all-girls plainsong choir floats above the congregation. A chorister's solo at the start contrasts with a congregation of nearly two thousand as they give voice to the great Advent hymns. The Canon Precentor, the Revd Tom Clammer, talks about how

> The human voice raised in song is extraordinarily powerful and perfectly expresses the emotion and expectation of Advent, a time when we begin the spiritual journey towards renewal. The candles are a moving symbol of new life and the procession a fitting expression of the pilgrimage through the year.[2]

'From darkness into light' represents the journey of a good Advent: the world is on a journey from darkness to light, and we rejoice in that light. We don't pretend that there isn't darkness, and the things that thrive in darkness and the horrors which it encompasses. But we know that darkness does not exist in itself: it is the absence of something – of light – so one light, one single light, shatters the darkness, however deep it is, and lights the way to itself.

Walking with those who have waited

As we walk through our Advent journey, we join with the lectionary readings which remind us that God's people are people who travel in hope waiting for his kingdom to be seen in full. For a good Advent it would be well for us to travel with them, the patriarchs, the prophets, John the Baptist and the Virgin Mary.

Speaking uncomfortable truth, especially to powerful people, was one of the key roles of the prophets. Some of them may, like Nathan, have been at court, among and consorting with the rulers. But no genuine prophet would merely have been of the establishment, saying what these people wanted to hear. The prophets were often the unwelcome voice of their religion; they were unpredictable, believing they were appointed by God. Their behaviour was marked by speaking poetically and using unfamiliar metaphors; by talking about the future and the intervention of God; and with the criticism of authority you find in Micah, in Isaiah, in Jeremiah and in many others down to John the Baptist many hundreds of years later. They were an unsettling presence, and so they were often unwelcome, frequently paying a high personal price for their vocation. They were crying out in conscience. It's as if someone is sitting on the shoulder of the people and shouting – look around you and see what is going on! Look at your society, look at your religion and look at your heart!

Their challenge to us in Advent is to ask ourselves, 'How do we use the power that we have? Our social relationships, our working structures, our use of wealth and influence, our politics and the systems of our society: do these things honour God or are they self-serving? Do we honour God with our lives or only with our lips?'

John the Baptist stood in the tradition of Isaiah's vision of God's kingdom, and he urges us to hold fast to an active and prophetic religion. That means promoting the practice of faith in all spheres of our life so that the light can break into the darkness and we can flourish as God's creatures. A faith which fails to shape our immediate world is essentially idle; a faith without action is worth nothing. Just like John it is our vocation as individuals and as the Church to witness to Christ. Karl Barth used the altarpiece in a church sanctuary in Isenheim, Germany, as a visual image of the role of the Church. It depicts the meeting of John and Jesus on the banks of the Jordan, with John's distorted index finger pointing to Jesus. In a single picture, we see the mission of the Church.

On the last Sunday of Advent we think about Mary as a forerunner, looking forward to the Incarnation and the reality that God incarnates not in a palace or through princes but through the powerless. The Methodist Contemporary Art Collection contains a piece by Jyoti Sahi, *The Dalit Madonna* (2000). The artist has sought to illuminate the Christian faith through the cultural traditions of India. The figure of Mary and her son, Christ, are seen in relation to the symbol of the grinding stone which can be found in every traditional Indian home and is often secured in the ground. The grinding stone consists of a mother stone which generally has a hollow centre into which fits a smaller seed- or egg-shaped stone, called the baby stone. This is free to move about and is used to grind various foodstuffs placed in the hollow of the mother stone. The stone remains at the heart of the home. In the picture, the grinding stone and baby stone are used to create an image of the Madonna with the Christ child (the baby stone) at her centre, almost in her womb.

Dalit is the current name for the caste previously called 'the untouchables'; it means 'broken'. Dalit women are oppressed because they are poor, because they are women and because they are Dalit, and this means that they often find themselves open to exploitation. When the picture was painted in 2000 it met with a great deal of shock – how could God choose such a woman? But he did. Although Mary was not an outcast she was from the lower parts of society – a refugee and unmarried. It is a powerful image that God is found among the broken and in unexpected places and people. A good Advent invites us to be people of hope, to find God in the broken parts of the world and see what is promised to us.

The role of the prophet is to speak not only into his or her generation but also into future generations of the promise of hope, and as we enter Advent we are called to a state of active waiting, to look back for what God has done and to look forward to the promise of hope. Above all, we are summoned to be active in the present moment – waiting in hope.

Waiting in hope

Hope is not about optimism: it is about a conviction concerning the future which leaps into our present in such a way that we feel secure in the here and now and ready for God's future, sure that he will save us, that the best is yet to come, that his kingdom of justice will triumph and he will judge us with mercy. We hope for a future where God's kingdom is in full; we hope for eternal life in which there is no more death and dying. Hope is stored up for us in heaven, and while it breaks into our present it is something that we wait patiently to see in full. Such is the word of promise and of hope. It is a message of God's unconditional love for all people. It is a promise which comes when we least expect it; it is a promise which will wipe away every tear. It is a promise of a future of justice, freedom, reconciliation and wholeness, but it is a promise which is seen by means of the recurring experience of redemption through time in the present.

In an Advent message to the Church in the province of South Africa in 2012, Archbishop Desmond Tutu spoke about how it was precisely in the darkness, where it looked as though there was no way forward, that the light which lightens everyone came into the world – and not an ideal world. Christ came into a world that was at war, was rife with injustice, into a people who were suffering pain and poverty. This is the reality of so many of us. And in the Incarnation God breaks in as shafts of sunlight through the clouds, with a promise that one day all will be light and God's glory will be fully seen. The light shines in the darkness and the darkness will not overcome it, and he will be our peace.

The language of hope, promise and waiting is not an easy one for today's culture. We don't always use the language of hope and have become more accustomed to the language of doubt and cynicism rather than expectation and promise. In a world where we have become accustomed to immediate and swift action, we don't like to wait, often seeking to eliminate all waiting. If we are going to have a good Advent we need to understand waiting. Waiting is not a passive act and Paula Gooder, in her book *The Meaning is in the Waiting* (Canterbury Press, 2008), in rediscovering waiting uses the example of pregnancy. In pregnancy waiting is anything but inactive. It is nurturing. It is full of hope and has value in its own right, and it is anything but passive.

To wait does not mean to pass the time with inactivity; a good Advent calls us to activity.

To be messengers

We are all called to serve as heralds of Christ's kingdom, to be messengers, as the prophet Isaiah says: 'How beautiful upon the mountains are the feet of the messenger who announces peace, who brings good news, who announces salvation' (Isaiah 52.7). In the words of the hymn by Edward Burns (born 1938),

> We have a gospel to proclaim,
> Good news for all throughout the earth;
> The gospel of a Saviour's name;
> We sing his glory, tell his worth.

We are to be messengers of the hope that God is present in his suffering world, that God's love is transforming the world and that the best is yet to come. But to be messengers of the good news can be a challenge; we live in times when people know little about the Christian faith. It is a time when the Christian narrative is forgotten and where the Church is too often in the media for the wrong reasons. To be messengers of hope we need to have a narrative which is relevant and is consistent in both word and deed.

When we ordain priests we are reminded that they are called with all God's people to tell the story of God's love. It has been said that storytellers are heart teachers. They unfold roads before us and behind us. They show us where the rough places are and where we might find good water. They accompany us as we walk through our own stories. Storytellers are those who build relationships – earning the right to be able to tell their story and the story of God's love. To have a good Advent we must be people who are messengers of hope, people who can tell our story of God's love.

To be the change we long to see

When we encounter others we need to do more than talk of God's love. We must demonstrate it in action and with integrity and with generosity. When Jesus was moved with compassion he told the story of God's love in word and in action – the lepers, made outcasts by their disease, were restored by his healing touch; the woman outcast because of her blood disorder was made whole by touch; those that were hungry were fed, the alien was welcomed and those lost like sheep without a shepherd were found.

In a good Advent we should know that we are called to action – to reach out to the hungry, the imprisoned, the homeless, the refugee, the naked, the sick and all those whom Jesus longs to touch – to become messengers of God's love. So as we wait for the kingdom of justice and righteousness we must become part of that change: speaking and living justice; reflecting God's love, wholeness and healing; being the peace that we long to see. The voice of Advent calls us to 'In the wilderness prepare the way of the LORD, make straight in the desert a highway for our God' (Isaiah 40.3). It calls us to proclaim justice, peace, righteousness, reconciliation and salvation. It calls us to be the light shining in the darkness.

To be people who know the hope to which we are called

If we are to be messengers of God's purpose of love and hope we need to be people who also experience this reality. We need to be people rooted in God and able to proclaim the words of the hymn 'I heard the voice of Jesus say' by Horatius Bonar (1808–89),

> I looked to Jesus, and I found
> In Him my star, my sun;
> And in the light of life I'll walk
> Till travelling days are done.

A good Advent is a time when we can wait with God, to be people who abide with him. We are used to developing Lent disciplines but we should also be people who develop Advent disciplines and spend time as disciples with God – waiting. How can we expect to see God and his light in the shadows if we do not turn aside and abide with him?

Ben Quash, in the Archbishop of Canterbury's 2013 Lent book *Abiding*,[3] talks about the importance of taking time to dwell more consciously and deliberately – this, he suggests, is the ability to abide. He uses the example of Moses' encounter with God in the burning bush in the book of Exodus and the fact that we are told twice that Moses looks at the bush. Moses 'looked, and the bush was blazing, yet it was not consumed. Then Moses said, "I must turn aside and look at this great sight, and see why the bush is not burned up"' (Exodus 3.2–3). First he looks, then he goes over and looks again, turning aside from his intended path. Once he has turned aside, God then addresses him. Moses hears his voice and he sees God.

If we want to be people of hope we need to be people who encounter God, who turn aside from our path and look and wait. Then we will have sight to see and can be formed into people of hope. Hope, as the author of the Hebrews reminds us (6.19), is an anchor for the soul, firm and secure. It is that which holds us when we are living in shadows.

When I was Canon Treasurer at Salisbury Cathedral I wore a purple cope, which was part of a set. My cope had an anchor on the back. I often commented, when there, that it was not as interesting as the other symbols my colleagues had on their copes – chalices, crosses and stars – but I came to understand that it was every bit as significant. The anchor is also seen in the *Window of Prisoners of Conscience* by Gabriel Loire at the east end of Salisbury Cathedral. The resplendent window reflects a Christian response to the violence and injustice so widely suffered in the twentieth century and commemorates prisoners of conscience of all races and faiths the world over. The presence of the anchor reminds us that it is hope which is the anchor of our soul. It is hope which holds us when we find our lives interwoven with the struggle between life and death, darkness and light – and hope which holds us in the face of the death and suffering in our own lives. A good Advent provides a time for us to find and know that hope of being rooted in and waiting on God. A good Advent prepares us for the rest of the year.

All creation straining on tiptoe

One of the wonderful things about Christmas is the look on children's faces as they see the Christmas tree light up, the lights across the high street or Father Christmas. And how often do we see them straining on tiptoes to get the best view? We seem as adults to lose our sense of anticipation and wonder. Maybe the heart of a good Advent is rediscovering that sense of expectation. In the words of the song written by The Fisherfolk,

> And all creation's straining on tiptoe just to see
> The sons of God, come into their own.[4]

Waiting, ready for action, and preparing everything in the house for Christ's arrival and listening out for his return. Peering like children on tiptoes just to see.

> Christ the Sun of Righteousness shine upon you,
> scatter the darkness from your path,
> and make you ready to meet him when he comes
> in glory;
> and the blessing of God almighty,
> the Father, the Son, and the Holy Spirit,
> be upon you and remain with you always.
> Amen.[5]

Notes

1 John Betjeman, 'Advent 1955', *Collected Poems*. London: John Murray, 2006.
2 <www.salisburycathedral.org.uk/news/new-star-%E2%80%98-darkness-light%E2%80%99>)
3 Ben Quash, *Abiding*. London: Bloomsbury Continuum, 2012, p. 65.
4 The Fisherfolk, 'On tiptoe', from the album *On Tiptoe*, 1975.
5 Blessing from *Common Worship: Services and Prayers for the Church of England*. London: Church House Publishing, 2000, p. 301.

A good Christmas

Rowan Williams

MASTER OF MAGDALENE COLLEGE

There are three kinds of Christmas carols.

The first kind of carol is basically summed up by 'Isn't it cold and shouldn't we be having a jolly time?' (For example, 'Jingle bells', 'I'm dreaming of a white Christmas', 'Deck the halls with boughs of holly'). The second kind of carol is 'Isn't the baby sweet?' ('Away in a manger' and 'Once in royal David's city'). But there is a third kind of Christmas carol which contains all sorts of rather disturbing, unusual and incomprehensible ideas and it is these that I want to focus on here.

In this third category, I'm thinking of things like the second verse of 'O come, all ye faithful' or indeed the second verse of 'Hark, the herald angels sing'. And, perhaps, rather surprisingly, 'We three kings of Orient'. Each of these may lead us to a way into thinking about what a good or Christian Christmas might involve our reflecting on.

The second verse of 'O come, all ye faithful' begins,

> God of God, Light of Light,
> Lo! he abhors not the Virgin's womb;
> Very God, Begotten, not created.

These densely packed, mostly fourth-century words still mysteriously retain a lot of popularity. What on earth are they saying? The second verse of 'O come, all ye faithful' is an attempt to answer the question, 'Who is at the centre of the Christmas story?' The answer is, 'It is the King of angels.' It is God who is at the centre of the story, and not simply God as such but 'God of God'. That is, God's life boiling over from eternity into time; God's life communicating itself so completely that it makes human life unrecognizably different. And when we've sung 'God of God' we go on to use one of the most ancient and powerful images for what that means, 'Light of light'.

The early Christian writers were deeply preoccupied with the search for images that would allow you to say that the life of God truly flows out from God into the world and yet leaves God undiminished. And what is that like? Well, like lighting a candle from another candle. Like a flame lit from a flame. There is no less of the first after you've lit the fire. God of God, Light of Light. Action, energy, that flows out from God and which is no less than God, because the God we believe in is a God whose very nature is to share life. There is nothing of God that is not sharing, nothing of God that is not giving, and God, the God we believe in as Christians, is a God who holds nothing back. That is the divine nature – God gives what God is. Very God, truly God, 'Begotten, not created' – because there is no beginning to this outflowing and boiling over that is the life of God in relation to us. There was no point at which it started, no point at which God said, 'Perhaps I ought to get out more.' From eternity, God bestows and gives, and it is in this flowing out of God's life that the world itself has its being, life, order and meaning. So that when at the end of all those carol services we hear the first verses of St John's Gospel about the Word that was 'in the beginning with God', the Word in whom was life, a life which was the light of humankind, it's all to do with the same set of themes.

So let's, for a moment, leave that insight to simmer on the Christmas stove and move on. We've seen that this carol celebrates a birth which is the beginning in our world of a life in which God is alive in a unique way. The God whose life and action is always just below the surface of our world breaks through like an underground stream gushing up at this moment in Bethlehem, two thousand years ago. Something begins for us. It's not the beginning of God being God, but it's the beginning of God being God like this in our hearts and minds. But this is where we flick forward in the pages to start singing 'Hark, the herald angels sing', because when God begins this life among us, when this birth happens that inaugurates a new way for God to be with us, God doesn't pick apart the fabric of the world and intrude like another person or another thing in the ordinary way. God works out the gift of divine life for us through a human life like ours.

> Veiled in flesh the Godhead see,
> Hail the incarnate Deity!
> Pleased as man with man to dwell.

Take away the obviously problematic 'man' language which we're all duly sensitized to these days, and what that verse says is 'God makes the difference by living humanly, as humanly as you and I do.' And that's an extraordinary claim. You would think, wouldn't you, that if God were going to act, God would do what we expect God to do, and in the words of the prophet, 'rend the heavens and come down'. Terry Eagleton, that great critic and philosopher and scourge of lazy-thinking agnostics, said, 'Some people seem to think that it would help if one day there was a large banner displayed in the sky saying, "I'm up here, you idiots."' God habitually works not by breaking into the world, but by filling out the world from within. So here we have that extraordinary affirmation, 'Pleased as man with man to dwell.' God delights to be human alongside human beings. In this life that begins at Bethlehem there is no little corner or gap where humanity breaks off and God starts. Everything is soaked through with the divine energy and love and light. This is the human life and, as another carol says, 'tears and smiles like us he knew'. In the pages of the Bible we read the same thing repeatedly. The Jesus we encounter in the New Testament is no superman. He asks, he weeps, he depends. We're told in the letter to the Hebrews that he feels tempted. His will sometimes appears to wobble like ours. There is a state of uncertainty and yet the life moves on, the decisions are made and the unbroken course and flow of God's life in Jesus continues.

God having made the world, in other words, doesn't interrupt it. God respects it and works within it. God changes things not by command or force exercised from outside, but God changes the world in its own terms and its own life. He changes the world by establishing human relationships which is, believe it or not, why the Church is still here. God redefines the capacities of human life:

Born to raise the sons of earth,
Born to give them second birth.

What's going on in this life, beginning in the stable, is that human capacity is being altered. What we can say and think and imagine about human beings has suddenly expanded beyond all measure. Here is complete divine creative freedom contained in a real vulnerable human life – 'born the king of angels', 'tears and smiles like us he knew'. 'God of God', 'Light of Light', 'Jesus wept'. Even in the baby in the manger absolute and creative freedom is alive, alive in a way that will animate and shape the whole of the human life that unfolds ahead.

This takes us to the third carol. God remakes, redefines human nature from within but does it by defenceless love and not by winning arguments or winning battles. Indeed, you might almost say by losing arguments and losing battles. 'If my kingdom came from this world,' says Jesus, 'my servants would be fighting.' And whenever you see Jesus' servants fighting you might reasonably conclude that the kingdom is of this world – but that's another story.

The carol 'We three kings of Orient', once you've separated it from the jolly knee-bending tune, contains all of this.

Glorious now behold him arise:
King and God and sacrifice.

God changes things by letting go. Instead of living out a life that is protected and successful in human terms, God lets go. Jesus entrusts himself to unreliable people like you and me. God puts his life, you could say, in the hands of fragile, tempted, muddled and fearful people. Whatever the details and whatever the fear, we are told unambiguously in the Christian Scriptures that it's Christ's exposure to pain and death and failure that somehow mysteriously makes the difference, makes the change that is affirmed in the resurrection from the dead and the giving of the Holy Spirit. This is a story which gives us a model of a God who will not use force upon us and a humanity that will not defend itself for its own sake.

We sing these carols with gusto year by year. We repeat these strange, lumpy, difficult words, we quote without realizing it from Pope Leo the Great and the *Te Deum Laudamus* and the Nicene Constantinopolitan Creed, and it doesn't do us any harm because these words, these somewhat mind-bending ideas, are what Christmas is about. What we celebrate at Christmas is not the birth of a particularly sweet and harmless baby, nor even the welcome possibility of having a few extra drinks in the middle of winter. We celebrate a set of discoveries about God and about humanity or, as Christians have regularly said, not so much discoveries as revelations. We are shown something about God.

We are shown that the God we believe in is not a God who has to be lured down from heaven by being very, very polite to him or behaving extra well. We are dealing with a God who can't help himself overflowing, boiling over into the world that he has made. This is a God who cannot give less than the life that is the divine life. We're dealing, in other words, with a God who doesn't have to be persuaded to be interested in us. That's quite a good start, and one way of keeping a good or Christian Christmas might be to look at what relics there are in our minds and hearts of an approach to God which still believes that God is essentially rather bored with us, rather removed from us and always in need of being kept sweet.

However long you've been a Christian or however long you've been looking wistfully at Christianity from outside, that's something which keeps obstinately coming back. I speak as a sinner to sinners, you understand. That something is deeply etched in our minds, the mythology of a God who somehow has to be persuaded to be on our side. You might as well try to persuade a waterfall to be wet. But there's more: the way in which that overflow impacts upon us is not by force or command, it's by a solidarity, an identification, so deep, so serious and total that we can only say when we see Jesus, we see God. And we see therefore, a God who values our humanity beyond all imagining.

Another way we might keep a Christian Christmas is to ask some awkward questions about how we value human lives, how we value the lives immediately around us, how we value the lives that impact upon us in negative, danger-ous and difficult ways. We continue to ask how we value the lives that appear not to be especially significant or effective or efficient. If we take seriously what these carols say we ought to be looking with speechless amazement at every human face. God thought this face was worth everything. God thought this person was worth everything. God thought, God thinks, that there is no gift or risk too great to bring full life and joy to this person. And God thought, and thinks, that this person can reflect something of the massive generosity that is God's own act of nature. It's possibly the hardest thing in the Christian faith to accept or understand, this radical sense that wherever we turn we see a humanity God has believed to be supremely worthwhile.

Of course, day by day, we make our little judgements and we take our sides. We think unthinkingly that such and such a life is obviously less worthwhile than another. We think the lives of our enemies are less worthwhile than the lives of our friends. And while there are monumentally difficult decisions to make in our world about the use of force, about defence and war and the like, the one thing the Christian has to be sure of is that, wherever we turn, the human life we see is a life as valuable as ours. If our actions diminish or destroy another life, that is nothing for triumph and all for tragedy. You could say that God's attitude to human nature is a bit like that of some master craftsman restoring an ancient and wonderful musical instrument. Looking at the old and damaged instrument the craftsman might say, 'Well, I could repair this with a bit of synthetic material, with a bit of composite here and a bit of glue there. But it's not actually going to perform what it's capable of performing unless I work very hard with the grain of the wood and replace what's worn out with the same material because that material is good and it's that material which is capable of singing.' So God approaches our humanity. God doesn't say, 'With a bit of luck I might find some moral, plastic substitute that will fill in the gaps.' God says that humanity itself needs to be inhabited and transfigured from within. So how do we look at that humanity? Even in its distorted, violent, threatening forms, even when we feel driven to those difficult decisions which now we face and the defence of our society?

And then the third question that comes about a Christian Christmas has to do with that last and hardest set of ideas. God's life overflows into our humanity. God inhabits our humanity fully in the life of Jesus, and then this inhabiting takes the form of an enormous risk-taking and letting go. This is an immense attention to the reality of the other, a defencelessness that we ought to find deeply frightening. A Christian Christmas is a time when we ought to be overwhelmed, both with the surprise of God's nearness and with the glory of the humanity that God restores, and at the same time alarmed, properly alarmed, by the radical nature of the claim made. If as children of earth we are to be raised and given a second birth, there is a letting go, a letting down of our defences against one another and against God which is the path to fullness of humanity – not very welcome and anything but easy, and yet mysteriously here we are singing about it (God help us!). And we only have the courage to sing about it, I dare say, because somehow or other we have begun to hear the good news of what kind of God our God is and the good news of what our humanity might be. And in the light of that, just maybe each of us is able to say that is a way, a life, which I want to be possible for myself and for the world.

So a Christian Christmas – a good Christmas – ought to be a very surprising time: a time when we look at our stale pictures and thoughts about God and about humanity and let them be refreshed by the newness of what comes into the world in Bethlehem. There is another carol, not popularly sung but often included in rather high-class carol concerts, that begins with the words 'A new work is come on hand'. A new work is come on hand, something becomes possible in our imagining of God and our imagining of humanity and of our own lives. As we sing and celebrate, the thing we ought most earnestly to pray for, this and every Christmas, is that we shan't lose the sense of surprise. The surprise that prevents us from thinking of God as a distant autocrat, the surprise that will prevent us from thinking of human beings as a sad lost cause or else as an absolutely successful and self-sufficient enterprise. God overflows in love and has trusted humanity to reveal the depth of divine life. That's not obvious and the surprising nature of it needs to be reaffirmed again and again. The whole point of Advent, that lost cause apart from chocolate calendars, is to give us a little bit of space to remember what it might be like not to believe all that, so that Christmas comes surprisingly. Even if Advent is a bit of a lost cause in our culture, that's no excuse for Christians not to try and clear the space, clear that room in the straw of the stable, as it were, to let themselves be amazed once again and to come and adore.

A good Epiphany

Libby Lane
BISHOP OF STOCKPORT

Some years ago a small child was standing in the hallway of her house, watching the Christmas tree with all its lights and decorations come down. When the rest of the house had been cleared, and the tree had been stripped and removed, the child remarked sadly, 'Christmas has gone out the door.'

The festival of Epiphany comes 12 days after Christmas, and for many it is linked to the putting away of decorations. It can sometimes feel rather cold and cheerless, a comedown after the excitement and drama of Christmas.

The best-known Epiphany poem, T. S. Eliot's 'Journey of the Magi', telling the imagined story of the journey of the 'wise men' to the infant Jesus, has a suitably bleak opening:

> A cold coming we had of it,
> Just the worst time of the year
> For a journey, and such a long journey:
> The ways deep and the weather sharp,
> The very dead of winter.[1]

The Magi themselves, delivering their gifts to Jesus, are often appropriated by the Christmas story, appearing in nativity plays and carols, such that their reappearance at Epiphany makes them seem like the guests who never leave as we attempt to blow the chilled embers of our hospitality back into grudging life.

For me, it is hospitality that lies at the heart of Epiphany, and it is a treasure. Stepping back from the dazzle and hustle of contemporary Christmas observance, it is in the marking of Epiphany, and the season that follows, that I find meaning and hope. In this short season we move from the manger to the cross, and answers can be sought to the questions of Jesus' birth, life and death, and 'What has this got to do with me?' A deeper examination of this season will, I hope, help us to revisit its profound and transformative themes, and engage in response to God's own act of hospitality towards us.

The visit of the Magi (Epiphany)

The 'wise men' of Eliot's poem are certainly uncomfortable. They have left behind their 'summer palaces on slopes' where 'silken girls' brought them sherbet. Instead the way is rutted and deep, the climate 'sharp'. The camels are bad-tempered, 'refractory', and they keep lying down in the slushy snow. The night-fires go out, the camel-men run away chasing liquor and women, there is no proper shelter, the locals are hostile and charge very high prices. Hospitality is at a very low ebb.

This is not the stately progress of visiting potentates. This is a descent into loss, disorientation, a losing of the way. In the ear of the narrator there is a voice constantly singing,

'This is folly.' He and his companions have 'no information'. Our own journey towards the 'Christ-event' – towards our own meeting with Jesus – can often feel like this: doubt and discomfort, an unsettling of our deepest self. We feel drawn, but we do not know where we are going. It feels foolish – leaving our familiar surroundings, our home comforts, to struggle with harsh conditions which may threaten our personal safety. And for what? An uncertain outcome at best. It is just not rational. It does not feel very wise.

Eliot's opening lines are a near quotation from Bishop Lancelot Andrewes, one of the foremost figures of the emergent Anglican Church in the Elizabethan era: a noted preacher, contributor to the translation of the King James Bible and much admired by Eliot for his ability to squeeze words until they yield a 'full juice of meaning'. In that spirit, we may note that Eliot, following Andrewes, places the word 'dead' in the middle of the last line of the opening section of the poem, 'The very dead of winter'. Epiphany comes in the middle of the dark, dead time of the year. Perhaps we are reminded of the words of the funeral service – 'In the midst of life we are in death.' Yet we are on the way to celebrate the birth of a baby, we are on the way to pay homage, as Matthew's Gospel puts it. In the poem, however, this purpose is blurred – are we seeing birth, or death? Rationally speaking, the evidence of our eyes was that a birth indeed took place, but it feels like death. We thought the two things were utterly different, but this birth is hard and bitter – in fact it is agony for us – and it seems to serve to remind us of our own death. For this is the inescapable fact of birth – it leads to death. And yet, as our wise man looks back on this hard journey towards death, he would do it again. What is to be found of such value in this bitter journey?

For Eliot's magus, his old home, his old 'place' – note the slippage from fine sun-kissed 'palace' to mere 'place' – is no longer enough, no longer satisfactory under the old dispensation, the old law, the old rule. The people seem alien, clutching at small 'g' gods who can do nothing to ease the agony, the sense of displacement. Another death, a death beyond the agony encountered on the journey, is something to be longed for. Is this the wise man's own death, or the death of another?

Once found, the place is, in Eliot's words, merely 'satisfactory'. Of course, the word picks up the echo of those 'refractory' camels. 'Refractory' means 'stubborn, obstinate, perverse; unmanageable, rebellious; strongly opposed; refusing compliance'. It might remind us of ourselves at times. 'Satisfactory', here, primarily means 'serving to make satisfaction or atonement for'. We think of the words of the Prayer of Consecration from the Book of Common Prayer, prayed by the priest over the elements of bread and wine:

> Almighty God, our heavenly Father, who of thy tender mercy didst give thine only son, Jesus Christ, to suffer death upon the cross for our redemption; who made there (by his one oblation of himself once offered) a full, perfect and sufficient sacrifice, oblation and satisfaction, for the sins of the whole world.

So in finding our satisfactory place, we find ourselves in fact at the foot of the cross.

T. S. Eliot wrote this poem in 1927, shortly after his conversion to Anglican Christianity. The poem is packed with Christian symbol and Anglican liturgy, but it is not what you would call enthusiastic. And yet, with its understatement, its gritty, determined resolution to recall and face the difficulty of belief, the discomfort and dislocation of it, it possesses an extraordinary beauty and a deeper comforting.

The death of the old ways – of thinking, of the power of reason, indeed the death of power itself – is accepted. For the magus in the poem, the possessor of knowledge, reader of the stars, the diviner of truths – all this is slipping away from him. He does not want it back. There is a deeper wisdom which begins with the acceptance that our power systems, our belief systems, our rationalities, even our religion, no longer fit us. They are no longer 'satisfactory', for they can no longer help us as they do not keep death at bay as we hoped they would. This acceptance is not in itself comfortable – if we turn to Christ looking for the recovery of our summer palaces we will be disappointed. We are invited to embark on a journey to a new home. We are asked to accept the darkness of the unknown, the adventure of the new; in other words, to accept change. The shedding of our old skins, the death of our old selves, the acceptance of our real death to come: these are sure signs of spiritual growth. It is notable that in the course of Eliot's poem there is no reference at all to the infant Jesus. The birth in question is our own 'rebirth'. This is 'the pearl of great price' hidden within the discomfort of the journey.

A good Epiphany, I think, is one which is first of all a journey to the foot of the cross, connecting the Christmas story with the Passion of Jesus. Our spiritual growth, with all the pains and trials attendant upon transformation, is planted in the soil of Golgotha. Of course, the Easter light of resurrection that nurtures our growth is part of Epiphany too, as we are led by the light of the star to discover the life of God made manifest among us. This is the light that makes the journey possible. God is the beginning and the end of our homecoming. Without the light of Christ we remain in darkness.

The Baptism of Christ (First Sunday of Epiphany)

Paradoxically, the journey both towards and away from the cross is one that is always being made by the Christian. As Martin Luther reminds us, we 'creep each day into our baptism'. That is to say that the process of transformation – or sanctification, in more traditional language – never leaves behind the cross and its significance for us. As we go further and deeper into the life of faith, there is no decrease in sinfulness as our sanctification increases. The two are always in tension. The Apostle Paul reminds us in Romans 7.19: 'For I do not do the good I want, but the evil I do not want is what I do.' Our journey is grounded so we do not begin to think that the purpose of our upward growth is to leave the world behind to live in a 'super-spiritual' continuum. This is the mistake the Corinthians made, for which they are upbraided by Paul: 'When I came to you, brothers and sisters, I did not come proclaiming the mystery of God to you in lofty words or wisdom. For I decided to know nothing among you except Jesus Christ, and him crucified' (1 Corinthians 2.1–2). Knowing that we too have been 'crucified with Christ', as Paul writes to the Galatians, we live out each day in the faith that Christ lives within us. Our growth comes as a sign of the work his Spirit is doing within us here and now, in the places and among the people where we live and work, in the ordinary everydayness of living. Our sphere of action, then, like Jesus' own, is this world, and how we choose to live in it.

A good Epiphany suggests that we should be spending time in prayerful preparation for a life in which discomfort in all its senses may come to us as a sign of our being 'born again'. One way of doing this is to take seriously the reaffirmation of our baptismal vows, making our baptism a present experience, not just a past event.

Jesus' own baptism marked the beginning of his public ministry. Matthew's Gospel gives some clues about why Jesus himself thought his own baptism was necessary. After all, as John the Baptist points out, it is to Jesus himself, the man without sin, that we come in repentance. Why would Jesus need to be baptized? The answer Jesus gives to John's question, 'And do you come to me?' is to insist that 'It is fitting for us to fulfil all righteousness.' Jesus in his humanity identifies with the condition of us all as sinners in need of repentance. He does not set himself apart, even though he was uniquely qualified to do so, but commits himself fully and utterly to seeking after the righteousness which is ushered in with the coming kingdom of God. This complete identification by Jesus with his Father's righteousness is affirmed by the 'epiphany' of the very Holy Spirit with which the promised Messiah will baptize. In reaffirming our turning to Christ in repentance, we invite the continuing work of the Holy Spirit in our own lives as we choose to dwell in Christ and he in us. Thus we are equipped to face the journey ahead, not in our own strength but resourced and empowered by that same Holy Spirit. When we experience the Holy Spirit's work in us in this way, we begin to discover at first hand the hospitality of God.

Our willingness to set out on the journey of Epiphany and to be changed by the work of the Holy Spirit is without any expectation of becoming more comfortable. We will find instead that we are becoming increasingly uncomfortable with our former ways of life and increasingly unsatisfied by their charms. We can expect to become increasingly detached from the attractions of seeking for and holding power for its own sake, and from the needful desire for 'worldly' position. We are no longer under our own sovereignty but under the sovereignty of Christ and, made one with him through baptism – sharing his death and resurrection as he shared our life and death – we travel deeper into his kingdom upon his roads and on his terms.

The Conversion of Paul (25 January)

Those terms may well prove to involve 'very high prices' for some of us – we cannot help but think of the Christians facing terrible persecution in many parts of the world. There is nothing new in this persecution. The early followers of Christ faced arrest and execution, mob violence and discrimination. A severe famine in Palestine in AD 47–48 left the church 'poor, hungry, miserable, excluded and abused', according to one scholar.[2] Christians were discriminated against by those who controlled famine relief, and in Jerusalem the system of mutual aid described in Acts 4 was insufficient.

Christians were as a result often in debt and frequently found themselves taken to court by those from whom they borrowed.

One of the principal architects of this persecution was a young man named Saul. We are told how, present at the stoning of Stephen, Saul 'approved' of the killing. Stephen's death follows from his speech to the council of the High Priest, having been accused of 'saying things against this holy place and the law'. Stephen's message to the council is uncompromising: 'You stiff-necked people, uncircumcised in heart and ears, you are for ever opposing the Holy Spirit, just as your ancestors used to do' (Acts 7.51). We can imagine how such a message enraged his listeners, and it must have touched something very deep in Saul, since he then embarked on a vicious career of 'ravaging the church' by entering the houses of followers of Jesus, 'dragging off both men and women' and committing them to prison (Acts 8.3).

The account of Saul's persecution of the church in Jerusalem hints at the powerful and violent reactions the message of Jesus can evoke, and we receive a clear sense of what it was like to live at the time as a follower of the Way: 'Saul, still breathing threats and murder against the disciples of the Lord', goes to the high priest and requests introductions to synagogues in Damascus, 'so that if he found any who belonged to the Way, men or women, he might bring them bound to Jerusalem' (Acts 9.1–2).

This zealously violent man, is, however, chosen by God as 'an instrument . . . to bring my name before the Gentiles and kings and before the people of Israel'. Paul experiences a powerful epiphany – a revelation – on the road to Damascus when the risen and ascended Jesus meets with him and stops him in his tracks. These 'reversals' are the way God surprisingly sometimes chooses to act, a pattern that stems from the 'great reversal' of the cross itself, in which the one who is without sin suffers a violent and humiliating death 'for the forgiveness of sins', as the service of Holy Communion puts it. Saul, or Paul as he becomes, will suffer greatly in the course of his ministry. This suffering is not a 'tit-for-tat' visiting upon him of the wrath of God but an entering into the suffering of Christ himself, a full identification with the way of the cross and the path of humiliation. Paul emphasizes, writing to the Corinthians, how his sufferings have led him to an utter dependence upon Christ, who revealed to him that: 'My grace is sufficient for you, for power is made perfect in weakness.' As a result, Paul can be content 'with weaknesses, insults, hardships, persecutions, and calamities for the sake of Christ; for whenever I am weak, then I am strong' (2 Corinthians 12.10). Elsewhere Paul is able to rejoice in his sufferings because, he says, they produce endurance, 'and endurance produces character, and character produces hope, and hope does not disappoint us, because God's love has been poured into our hearts through the Holy Spirit that has been given to us' (Romans 5.4–5).

Throughout the New Testament, Christians are enjoined not only to endure their sufferings but to rejoice in them because they strengthen a hope in God's plans for his creation. This hope is strengthened in suffering because we are able to experience an outpouring of love as a gift of the Holy Spirit, of God being with us, as will be our experience for eternity when we are with God face to face. This outpouring of love leads us into the 'deep theme' of Epiphany – the hospitality of God.

The wedding at Cana
(Second Sunday of Epiphany)

When Paul witnessed the death of Stephen, he would have heard Stephen's remarkable last words: 'Lord, do not hold this sin against them.' A man suffering a violent death has a prayer of forgiveness on his lips. Perhaps this was the seed planted in Paul which led to his extraordinary ministry. Stephen was living out, to his last breath, Jesus' injunction to 'love your enemies and pray for those who persecute you'.

Underpinning the moral thinking of the ancient world was a principle of 'equivalence', which invites me to treat you in the way that I would expect to be treated by you. In the same way, if you treat me badly, then the principle invites me to treat you badly in return. Sometimes referred to as the Golden Rule, this is the basis for systems of law and justice which seek to keep the peace by maintaining an equilibrium between parties. It is the basis for retributive punishment and compensation and the licence for retaliation in the face of an attack. In Matthew's Gospel Jesus directly addresses this way of thinking:

> You have heard that it was said, 'An eye for an eye and a tooth for a tooth.' But I say to you, do not resist an evildoer. But if anyone strikes you on the right cheek, turn the other also.   (Matthew 5.38–39)

Jesus overturns the Golden Rule and introduces a new, radical perspective on human relations and community ties based on forgoing one's rights of retaliation.

However, Jesus goes even further, overturning not only the retributive side of the Golden Rule but the more positive side too, the side which leads me to expect a return in exchange for a gift or a good deed: 'You have heard that it was said, "You shall love your neighbour and hate your enemy." But I say to you, love your enemies and pray for those who persecute you' (Matthew 5.43–44). Jesus is introducing the values of the kingdom of God to traditional human wisdom. These values are very risky if preservation of equilibrium is the goal. They may lead to loss and humiliation. 'If you love those who love you, what reward do you have? . . . And if you greet only your brothers and sisters, what more are you doing than others?' (Matthew 5.46–47).

Jesus challenges us to move beyond the easy exchanges of equivalence to embrace the 'less' – the possibility of loss, of not getting back what we give – because this, paradoxically, is the way to receive the 'more' that God has in store. In Luke's Gospel, we find an additional thought that illuminates the point still further: 'But love your enemies, do good, and lend, expecting nothing in return . . . Give, and it will be given to you. A good measure, pressed down, shaken together, running over, will be put into your lap' (Luke 6.35, 38).

This image of plenty, brimming over, of 'good measure', this 'more' that God gives, is nowhere manifested more surprisingly and dramatically than the transformation of water into wine at a wedding party in Cana, as told in John's Gospel. How typical of the style of Jesus' generous hospitality to solve a problem quietly and undemonstratively so as to preserve the host's dignity and please his guests, leaving everyone free to taste something better than they could have hoped for. It is important, though, to link this image of joyful and surprising abundance with the 'more' that Jesus asks us to do in loving our enemies.

The French philosopher Paul Ricoeur calls the command to love one's enemies the 'logic of superabundance' and it lies at the heart of what he calls 'the economy of the gift'. 'The enemy', says Ricoeur, 'becomes the touchstone of the new ethics, the criterion of its universality; love is boundless, in the same way as vengeance, at the opposite end of the trajectory, was limitless!'[3]

What underlies this perspective is the idea of God's original gift of creation in which every good thing is given to humanity as an act of generosity. It is in God's character to be generous, kind and merciful, even (or especially) towards the ungrateful, which includes all of us. In responding to the call to love our enemies, we are participating in the generous nature of God and setting aside the self-interest implicit within the human logic of equivalence. To live generously, therefore, is to respond to an initial act of generosity on the part of a God who forgoes the privileges of the divine and comes towards us and lives among us, ultimately suffering and dying 'for us'.

The 'boundlessness' of God's love for all creation invites us to live extravagantly – like those Magi, to wander across 'bounds' and borders, not as invaders and crusaders but as bringers of gifts: of mediation, of peace, of friendship and solidarity. These borders may be within our own communities and neighbourhoods, indeed within our own households, as much as across wider national and international perspectives. There is no one who is not included in or connected to God's hospitality. This involves considerable risk, but we do it not in a triumphalist spirit of conquest in which we try to overcome the hostility of our enemy, but in the spirit of Jesus' command to love and pray for those who persecute us.

This perspective is sometimes understood as weak and unappealing, criticized at the personal level for leaving people who are oppressed languishing in their suffering and being told to bear it humbly and, at the level of international conflict, accused of being ineffective in the face of tyranny and evil. It is seen as justification, for example, for slaves remaining enslaved, for women remaining disenfranchised and disempowered, or for victims of abuse to remain in bad relationships.

However, the putting aside of our own interests and renouncing the claim to our own privileges is applicable only after the manner of Christ, who took the form of a servant (Philippians 2.6ff.) by free choice rather than because he had no choice. It is not Christ-like to be compelled by violence, threat or coercion into submission. God's will, rather than our own perspective, and his generous initiating movement towards us may thus become the basis for standing in and acting upon the world. Far from being subjugated, the Christian is able to make the surprise move, the disarming gesture, because she is not defending her own interests but living out of the source of all strength and authority. The heart of a good Epiphany, then, is a realization of the 'surprise move' God makes towards us in his abundantly generous self-giving.

Beyond personal loving and forgiving, the universal Church, the body of Christ on earth, is called to act out of God's generosity and never out of its own interests. The Church is to be active custodian of hospitality and generosity – holding open a space for warring interests to step back and find peaceable ways of resolving conflict; advocating for the poor of the earth, the hungry and the destitute and upholding the dignity of each and every human life, no matter how valueless they appear to others; seeking for justice and holding to account the oppressors. Generous self-sacrificing love seeks not to ignore injustice but to uphold the justice of God.

The need for justice reminds us, however, that the generosity and hospitality of God goes beyond the human justice of equivalence. Paul Ricoeur suggested that the 'logic of superabundance' transforms and transfigures the logic of equivalence and makes it possible to imagine a world in which all are invested in the good of the other. Human justice may be needed in a world in which our imaginations are incomplete, in which we fail to see and act upon another's need, but at the heart of the justice of the kingdom of God lies a mercy of which the lack of measure is its main characteristic – that overflowing measure, that extravagant gift, that flourishing life that transforms the mechanics of 'mere reciprocity' into something wonderful. The command to love one's enemies is disorienting – disorienting of oneself, as Eliot's magi suggest, and disorienting to those with whom one engages. Yet through this disorientation comes a reorientation into a new place of mutual creative possibilities.

The Presentation of Christ or Candlemas (2 February)

There is a church in one of the poorer parts of the diocese of Chichester that has been giving support to a small number of the Syrian refugees who have arrived in the UK. One of them is a woman whom I recently confirmed. An Iraqi Christian married to a Syrian, she had lived in Syria and prior to the troubles she was abandoned by her husband, who took her children and left her to fend for herself. Vulnerable to ethnic and religious 'cleansing' she was rescued by a United Nations mission and taken to a camp in a neighbouring country before coming to the UK. She found deep wisdom and solace in the Lord's Prayer. Asked whether she hated her 'enemies', she said that her task is to forgive those who persecute her. It is for God to deliver her from evil. She sees her 'deliverance' by the UN mission, and by those who have given her support and shelter since her arrival in the north of England, as God at work in her life.

Her story connects many of the themes we have encountered on the journey through Epiphany: coming to the foot of the cross; the hospitality of God we find there; the super-abundance of God's love for us as the basis for our own forgiveness of our enemies; receiving 'all of God' and his righteousness in baptism. All these themes have pointed us towards 'epiphany' – a realization of who Jesus is. That recognition lies at the heart of the story and liturgy which marks the conclusion of Epiphany, the presentation of Christ in the temple.

This courageous woman's testimony connects her to another female prophet, Anna, hidden in the shades of the Jerusalem temple, who slips briefly into history to bear witness to the child Jesus and his true identity.

Anna was a woman of very great age who, we are told, never left the temple but worshipped there, fasting and praying, day and night. The day Mary and Joseph brought Jesus to the temple for presentation, the Holy Spirit led an elderly man, Simeon, to come to the temple too. He had had his own epiphany – the revelation that he would not see death until he had set eyes on the Lord's Messiah. Simeon is described as a man 'looking forward to the consolation of Israel' and in the power of the Spirit he identifies the child Jesus as the bringer of that salvation.

Simeon's song is all about epiphany – about revelation: Jesus is to be 'light for revelation to the Gentiles'. This is an astonishing claim to be made about Israel's promised Messiah, thought to be the restorer of Israel to its former pre-eminence, but also a recapitulation of Israel's vocation in Exodus 19 as a 'holy and priestly nation'. But it is given to a woman, the prophet Anna, to be the one who immediately shares this revelation with those who are gathered outside the inner sanctum: Anna 'began to praise God and to speak about the child to all who were looking for the redemption of Jerusalem' (Luke 2.38).

Anna, we may say, was the first evangelist, and the Syrian confirmand, in testifying to her 'deliverance' and practising forgiveness of those who have sinned against her, brings the Epiphany, to which Anna originally testified, right into our midst today.

A good Epiphany starts with a journey embracing discomfort, loss and death, bringing us from the vulnerable baby in the stable to the dying young man on the cross. What is made manifest in Jesus is the 'superabundance' of God's generosity. It is on the solid ground of that generosity that we as Christians are able to act in the world – loving enemies not in a metaphorical way, but in a self-sacrificing, practical way, working for peace, working for justice, loving and forgiving 'because he first loved us'. Christmas has indeed 'gone out the door' and, in making the journey of a good Epiphany, we go with it to share the good news with others.

Notes

1 T. S. Eliot, 'Journey of the Magi', *Collected Poems 1909–1962*. London: Faber & Faber, 1974.
2 D. L. Mealand, *Poverty and Expectation in the Gospels*. London: SPCK, 1980.
3 Paul Ricoeur, 'The Golden Rule: Exegetical and theological perplexities', *New Testament Studies* 36 (1990), pp. 392–7.

A good Lent

Justin Welby
ARCHBISHOP OF CANTERBURY

Some things stick in the memory. In 2004, while I was working at Coventry Cathedral, I visited a part of Africa which was in the midst of some very serious fighting. A group of black-clad militias was moving across the area, killing, looting, burning.

With a colleague I drove into the area where the fighting was going on, to a small town that was under siege, or had been. On the way there, after a long period in the car on very bad roads, we stopped for a few moments' break. There was a series of burnt huts to our right, and I walked a few metres towards them.

Around me rose ash. In fact, it was the Monday before Ash Wednesday. The ash rose in clouds, settling on me, from the burnt houses, and as I walked I realized the ash came from those who had been burned.

That was ash without hope, ash without change, ash rising in clouds to call all who saw it to acknowledge human evil but not to promise anything better.

Every Ash Wednesday when I'm at a service with the ashing, it's that ash that comes back to my mind, and I see in my mind's eye again, the small bumps in the ground where people had been killed, the marks of blood upon the walls, the destroyed huts.

Ash Wednesday is a moment in which we are called afresh to look at the reality that that village represented – the reality that is the reality of human sinfulness and evil – and to reflect that that lies deeply within ourselves, all of us without exception. Not perhaps to that extent, but in one way or another.

A good Lent takes hold of that and, in an extraordinary way, makes space for the hope of Christ. It makes space for the hope of Christ not only in our own individual lives but also in the life of the household and family, in the life of the Church and of local communities and, I would suggest, in the life of society generally.

I want to reflect on how this works through some words from an Old Testament prophet and the writings of a sixth-century monk: the prophecy of Isaiah and the Rule of St Benedict.

Recently I visited Bishop Angaelos, the remarkable Coptic Bishop in Britain, to condole with him on the loss of lives in his community, on the terrible killings of Coptic Christians in Egypt, and he told me some of the details. I won't tell you all of them, but there is one that is extraordinary.

The Christians were given the opportunity to convert and chose not to, knowing the consequence, and then they were killed, most terribly. And the one who got away tells that each of them, as they were killed, was calling out, 'Jesus is Lord.'

A good Lent makes space for the hope of Christ in a way that draws us into their fellowship and to walk with them. Isaiah 40.3 says: 'A voice cries out: "In the wilderness prepare the way of the Lord, make straight in the desert a highway for our God."' The prophet Isaiah speaks to a people in exile and despair – much how many Christians across the Middle East and Africa must be feeling right now, and in other places too – offering them hope and return and a purpose.

The way in which that return will be experienced by the Jewish people coming back from Babylon to Israel, the way that they are going to experience that, covers every aspect of their life together – from the individual to the national – and draws in the decisions of their imperial masters, especially Cyrus, the Persian king.

Over the following 27 chapters of Isaiah, the exiled and those returning will find an extended justification by God of his judgement on the people – and a consequent call for holiness, and for place to be made in their lives and in their way of living that means the blessing of his presence is fully experienced. A good Lent makes space for the presence of God in all.

But Lent is probably one of the most individualistic of the great Christian seasons, at least in our modern way of doing it. The question of 'What are you doing for Lent?' is always one which is asked with an implicit singular 'you'. In French it would be '*tu*' rather than '*vous*'. But actually we have to stop seeing Lent, if it is to be a good Lent, simply as something that is individual.

The House of Bishops' Pastoral Letter, published on Shrove Tuesday 2015, has at its heart that tension between the individual and the joint. It contrasts the solitary stranger and the community of communities. It calls for a moral vision of society in which every level is brought into forms of relationship that are healthy, energizing and lead to human flourishing. It is neither left-wing nor right-wing. It notes the absence of a capacity for moral debate in this country; it puts the way we live on a spectrum not of left and right, but of holiness and sin. A good Lent makes space for hope by leading us afresh into encounter with the holiness of God. The central point of that Pastoral Letter is that human beings are made to live in relationship, and communities of human beings are made to live in relationship with other communities.

In Lent, we are not to turn inwardly to ourselves, but to start with ourselves and to see a transformed life in community and relationship, not only with God but with each other. It's not a *tu*, it's a *vous*. It's not what are 'you' doing (singular) but what are 'you' doing (plural) that Christ puts to us.

The key response in relation to God's hope to the exiles comes near the very end of Isaiah (65.1), where the highway of God's promised return is realized in God's own words to the people. When God says to them, almost desperately: 'Here I am, here I am.'

These are words that would echo loudly for Isaiah, because they are the very words he voiced to God at the very start of his ministry (6.8 – 'Here I am; send me'). The individuality of Isaiah's Lenten call – 'Here I am; send me' – is magnificently reversed into a universality by which God is available, and longing to draw near, to his people. God calls to us, and to each of us, continually. Our response must above all be to listen and to pay attention. In listening, the doors of hope are opened afresh. God says to the returned exiles of Israel: 'When I called, no one answered, when I spoke, they did not listen.'

In the Rule of St Benedict, Benedict says in his introduction: 'Let us hear with awestruck ears what the divine voice, crying out daily, doth admonish us'; and also: 'What, dearest brethren, can be sweeter to us than this voice of the Lord inviting us?'

So for each of us a good Lent begins with paying attention, with beginning to make straight the way of the Lord by listening. Listening begins with Ash Wednesday. We have to start by acknowledging our sin and our humanity. We cannot listen while we fill our ears with our own self-confidence and our own self-worth. What we are is what we are in Christ, and nothing more. And what that is is the summit of all God's creation: flawed and fallen in sin, but with all the possibilities which our Saviour brings us.

Each of us, in Christ, is saved from slavery to sin and the condemnation that goes with it. We are saved for the delights of walking with Christ in relationship. Of being drawn into his global family. Into the great purpose of bringing in the kingdom of God so that the world may see the glory of Christ and find itself the unmeasurable and surpassing joy of serving God and being embraced by his love. In Lent we open the way of hope, that the world may see.

We used to be a lot tougher about this. Today, Lent is a form of self-improvement, if it is observed at all. Someone said a few days ago that nowadays it tends to consist of giving up sugar in coffee or doing without your biscuit. I'm not sure what it achieves, but it is infinitely more than that. At the individual level it draws us to see what we have been saved from and what we are being saved for.

With a slight sense of mischief, I have reintroduced the idea that we say the Commination from the Book of Common Prayer at Lambeth Palace on Ash Wednesday, as is prescribed in the Rubric. It starts with an initial cursing of all kinds of interesting things like removing our neighbour's landmark, as well as rather more serious modern sins like perverting the judgement of the stranger, the fatherless and the widow, and so on and so forth. Towards the end it says this (I'm only telling you, not because I assume you don't know the Commination by heart, but because the words have a certain resonance, even though you will have said them many times):

> Although we have sinned, yet have we an Advocate with the Father, Jesus Christ the righteous ... let us therefore return unto him ... and be ordered by the governance of his Holy Spirit; seeking always his glory and serving him duly in our vocation with thanksgiving.

This is a bit more serious than indicated by giving up a biscuit with one's coffee.

So what do we do for a good Lent individually?

We listen. We listen to the voice that echoes through creation, the voice that cries to each of us: 'Here I am, here I am.' What does that mean in practice? One of the wonderful things about Scripture is that it is there that we listen, whether we are listening to it in a service in a liturgical setting or reading a few words before we go to sleep.

And we need to remember that the words of Scripture were not written by people in comfortable circumstances far from the distractions of life, but in the midst of all the terrors and horrors that we see still lived out today in the same areas of the Middle East. Those who wrote it knew what it was to be a refugee and slave, they knew persecution and genocide. For that reason, as we turn to its pages and seek the Spirit of God, we will find comfort and hope.

But let us be practical. For those who have incredibly busy lives, with long hours – and many work in offices where there is not a single moment of silence or space during the day, and I do remember that. For those who leave early for work, who are not in control of their diary and the events with which they deal, and return late and tired. For those who are carers at home, isolated, often lonely, with many demands. For those who are housebound by illness. For all the different categories. For those who amid it all strive to maintain some kind of life in a household, time with partner and children or friends, developing some hinterland beyond the demands of daily life.

For all of them, listening is so difficult. So, how do we listen? Let me suggest one Lent discipline which you might like to add to giving up the biscuit.

Read Luke's Gospel, taking a small chunk each day, and ask yourself as you read it three simple questions: What does it say? What does it mean? What am I going to do about it? Very simple.

What does it say? This first question is simply an exercise in putting ourselves into the place of the listener or the observer. In Caravaggio's picture of the call of Matthew, where a rich group of tax collectors sit behind a table, Jesus, in bare feet, comes in. He points to Matthew, who looks astonished. Matthew points to his own chest; he can't believe he's been singled out: 'What, me? You want me?' Peter's behind him ... not quite daring to point himself. Where are you in that picture? Fr Laurent Fabre, the founder of Chemin Neuf, says: 'I'm Matthew, that's who I am. I'm the one who is far away, every time I look at him.' Where are you in the story?

What does it say? What's going on? What does it mean? People are intimidated by the Bible, wondering if they shouldn't see something immensely profound. The answer is that you see what God shows you on the day. Sometimes you see a lot, sometimes you see a little. If you have a short time, ask yourself the obvious questions about the plain meaning of the text before you. Of course there is more, of course one can learn New Testament Greek and read profound commentaries, and that is wonderful. But in Lent, do what you can, not what you can't.

What do I do about it? Ask yourself: 'How do I make my life more open to Christ because of what this is saying to me?'

For myself, such reading is part of my own daily discipline of prayer, which includes a lot of other things as well. Time is spent and at the end of jotting down whatever banal or very occasionally less banal thoughts I have, I always put in a couple of lines of what I can do in response to those thoughts. Sometimes it is very practical, writing to someone or speaking to someone who I may have offended. It may be very simple, merely saying a prayer of sorry or thank you, or a petition for something of which I need reminding. Of course, to make straight the way of the Lord, so that he comes to us, to open our lives so that hope comes up fresh, to smooth out the road so that our lives are open to listening, has infinitely more variety than this.

Let me suggest one other. As individuals, even short periods of complete silence during Lent, fasting from noise and, How little we do of it.

Every weekday at Lambeth Palace, in the Chapel, there is a period of silent prayer after Evening Prayer. When I can, I join with the community there in the silent prayer.

It starts with my mind churning with the happenings of the day and forthcoming events, with reports in the press, with resentments and joys, and the occasional twinge of cramp in my foot. Fortunately, I am not the only one and silence is occasionally disturbed by an 'ouch' and a shifting. But as the churning subsides, I begin to hear other things. The sound of a siren going by (we live between a police station, a fire station and a hospital). Then after a while I incorporate that into the prayer and find, just a little, that God is in the midst, and space is being made and I can hear.

I've had to learn, and I'm still very much learning, that I do not need to do anything in that time. I need only to be willing to listen. It is a time of meditation and reflection, of discovering the God who – all the time – is saying: 'Here I am.'

But Lent is no mere individualistic, narcissistic and inward-looking self-help festival. The basic building block of society has been communities of different sorts and shapes. What that means has varied extensively at different ages and in different places. For many people it is still a family, that wonderful building block of society: one of many. For others it's an extended family, for others a group of friends you see most regularly or with whom you share a house. A good Lent must overflow in generosity. It's one of the signs.

Here again, take out the bumps in the road. How do we live a good Lent with those we live with? What are the bumps in the road we need to smooth out for the Lord to come? What are the relationships that have been neglected and therefore are full of clutter that needs removing? They can be very difficult: broken relationships may be easily mendable little irritations – or it may be that we need, in a good Lent, to take the first step to clearing away a major landslide.

The Community of St Anselm, based at Lambeth Palace, has as part of its prayer discipline the process of confession with one another, of being open with one another in prayer. I've watched them do it at Chemin Neuf too; it's not a lot of laughs, sitting with someone you live with, having to confess where you've gone wrong. But it doesn't half make for functional community. We need to deal with what it is we find in those closest to us . . .

How do you do it in practice? Openness, transparency, and also going back and using the same approach to Scripture as I suggested a few moments ago. One has to treat each person and situation differently.

There's a wonderful book called *The Pastoral Rule of Gregory the Great* which describes this at great length. If you're going to deal with relationships, if you're going to smooth the road so God finds a living community of those who love one another and shine out and overflow with the goodness of Christ, you'll have to deal with each person individually.

Look at the story of Zacchaeus. The story is dramatic enough and also extremely humorous. Its events will have shocked the crowd that watched them. Here was a bad guy, a tax collector, received by Jesus – who knew his name – who then invites Jesus to his home (and Jesus accepts) and repents and turns away from all he does wrong. What we have here is a series of mended relationships. Zacchaeus repairs his relationship with the community of Israel. With Jesus he makes a new relationship, and he sorts himself out with God. His household will have been turned into a place of hospitality rather than extortion. That is a good Lent, lived in a few hours in Jericho on a hot day.

The bigger the institution we are part of, the harder it is to have a moral centre that is maintained, and the easier it is to slip into bad habits with institutional life that drown out the voice of God. That has always been an issue with the Church, and remains an issue today. Our own concerns and troubles, even the entirely legitimate ones, may obscure our capacity to see and hear Christ in those with whom we disagree. A really good Lent, for the Church moving outwards again, is one in which we give up not listening.

We may also give up insisting that everything must be done for us and in our way. We may even take up the habit of paying attention to those we find difficult and with whom we disagree.

Making space for Christ in the life of the Church comes when the Church looks outwards and suddenly he is there in our midst. The discipline of a good Lent is to find again how we welcome the stranger, how we practise hospitality, how we listen. We hear in the most unlikely places when we listen collectively. Benedict reminds us that

> whenever weighty matters are to be transacted in the monastery, let the Abbot call together the whole community . . . we said that all should be called for counsel, because the Lord often reveals to the younger what is best.[1]

It is the eternal experience of the Church that God's word to us comes in surprising ways and from unusual, and very often, in our eyes, unimportant people. In practice, let us see whether together we cannot make a discipline of listening better; and perhaps in churches gathering once or twice during Lent for a period of prayer, of silence, of confession, of dealing with bad relationships and of sharing a meal together. There we will find Christ. There the road will be made smoother.

And I just want to end by imagining for a moment whether it is possible to have a good Lent in society as a whole. Can we even talk of such?

It is the point for which we pray, 'your will be done on earth, as in heaven', and like all prayer we need to follow that prayer by saying inside ourselves, 'Here am I; send me.' It is where we find God's Spirit at work in the world: both where the world breaks into the life and action of the Church, and where the Church breaks into the life and action of the world.

The Bishops' Letter talked of the need of a new politics. Perhaps that new politics includes the capacity to listen humbly to one another – which we find so difficult – to serve and form new exercises of power. To create and make space for people to flourish, to grow their own businesses, to hold solidarity, to make space for those who are weak to bless the strong. To make straight the way of the Lord, to let justice roll down like waters, and righteousness like an ever-flowing stream.

The interaction of Church and society is the foundation of a good Lent and a good Lent the foundation of a just society. Not a Lent of abstinence, but a Lent of listening to our vocation, of rejoicing with those for whom things are going well, of suffering with those left behind. A listening Lent is one of robust disagreement – not bland assurance, but disagreement with a moral vision and destination.

A good Lent starts within us. It moves through those most closely around us. It comes into the Church and it must be so generously experienced that it overflows into society. We will not really have a good Lent until that chain is complete, and for that we pray, 'may your kingdom come'.

Note

1 The Rule of St Benedict, chapter 3.

A good Holy Week

Stephen Cottrell
BISHOP OF CHELMSFORD

That was the day they killed the Son of God
On a squat hill-top by Jerusalem.[1]

So begins Edwin Muir's stark and beautiful poem, 'The killing', and it is also a good place to begin a conversation about Holy Week, because Holy Week is nothing if it is not a journey to the cross. In the poem all sorts of people come to the cross, 'the hardened old and the hard-hearted young', though in the end they are disappointed by death and feel cheated. It was not the spectacle they hoped for. Only the women wait patiently, watching, not moving all day. And the poem ends with a question:

Did a God
Indeed in dying cross my life that day
... he on his road and I on mine?

When the liturgies of Holy Week work well we are converted. Holy Week is a parish mission every year, drawing us back to the central truths of the Christian faith and to the cross itself. We are challenged to stop and watch and wait. We are reminded of our own death, of our entanglement in *this* death and of its implications for our lives. We are invited to respond. And *how* we celebrate Holy Week, and how many people join in, is itself a sort of spiritual barometer for measuring the health of the Church. For if we will not come to the cross, what else are we avoiding?

Holy Week draws us back and draws us in. Like a great work of art, the liturgies of Holy Week present the story of the Christian faith as a participative drama. And because the Christian faith is always a story before it is a statement, so the creed itself is deconstructed by the liturgy: laid out and populated through the liturgical drama, and then put back together as a narrative for life in which we are the players on the stage, not just the spectators in the stalls. This is how all liturgy works. This is how belief is inhabited.

I have four suggestions:

1 Attend everything.
2 Go for broke.
3 Punctuate the liturgy with other voices.
4 Pay attention to the space between the notes.

And if you want to develop or even begin to do Holy Week in your parish then the resource book you need is *Common Worship: Times and Seasons*,[2] though these liturgies rest of course on the ancient practice of the Church.

So, first of all, attend everything. I know this is difficult in a frantic society like ours, but there are far too many Christians who sing 'Hosanna' one Sunday and 'Alleluia' the next, but do not come and stand at the cross. This distorts Christian witness and helps us to avoid the uncomfortable realization that Jesus was not killed by wicked men (as the old Prayer Book Collect has it) but by very good and ordinary men and women like us. By religious people who got it wrong. The 'good' people who sang 'Hosanna' and greeted Christ with joy on Sunday were the same 'bad' people who bayed for his blood on Friday. Therefore, when we enter into the whole drama of Holy Week we begin to see how we are implicated in the events. Our muddled motives and our misunderstandings are exposed. Therefore we must make every effort, and encourage other people to make every effort, *to attend*, to be there. As Woody Allen famously observed, 90 per cent of life is turning up. So turn up. Just be there and be part of it, and see where you are taken.

One of the best ways of doing this is to teach and encourage people to see Holy Week not as four services but *one*: one incredible liturgical drama spread over the four days of Palm Sunday, Maundy Thursday, Good Friday and Easter Day. And just as you wouldn't dream of booking tickets for *Hamlet*, watching Act 1, slipping out for some shopping and a lie down during Acts 2, 3 and 4, and then coming back for Act 5, so it should be unthinkable that you would miss the central drama of Maundy Thursday and Good Friday and just return for Easter. If you do, Easter itself is diminished. It is no longer the climax of a drama, the unfolding of God's purposes where cross and resurrection are part of a single salvation story, and where in washing feet and breaking bread Christ himself provides the hermeneutical key to all that follows; rather, it is an isolated happy ending in a story robbed of pain and grief, and therefore also robbed of meaning and joy. There is something rather empty about singing 'Alleluia' if you've never been to the cross. It is like singing the national anthem of someone else's country. The words and the tune may be correct. But there's no substance to the song.

Thinking of Holy Week as *one* service rather than four also helps those churches who (in my view mistakenly) feel they are somehow letting the side down if they don't *anticipate* Easter in their Maundy Thursday and Good Friday services. So there are churches where they will have some sort of liturgy of the Passion but feel obligated – almost as a show of faith – to add some Easter declaration at the end, something to cheer us all up. Rather, and as I shall say in a little while, the invitation is to experience the desolation and emptiness of the cross. The whole point is that we do not and cannot sing 'Alleluia' yet. After all, Holy Saturday is the one day of the year where there is no water in the font, no sacrament in the tabernacle, no Eucharist offered. We just ache and wait. And it is this aching and waiting that give Easter its joy and meaning. Only when we begin to experience Christ as dead can we celebrate the joy and surprise of him risen.

So how do we celebrate these services? Well, we go for broke. Or as Mae West put it: 'If you've got it, flaunt it!' This seems to me to be a good approach to liturgy. In the services of Holy Week, we have most certainly got it – a beautiful and compelling set of services – but we don't always flaunt it. Our offerings are sometimes pinched and mean. We need, rather, to revel in the sensuous and very hands-on re-enactment of liturgical drama. Think of Holy Week as an opera (an art form which is itself a heady blend of poetry, drama and music), and think of Palm Sunday as the overture. In the liturgy of Palm Sunday the story of Holy Week begins. Jesus' entry into Jerusalem is re-enacted.

So make your Palm Sunday procession mean something. Don't start at the gate and shuffle a hundred yards or so to the church. Don't do a figure of eight on the inside of the building, but seize the opportunity to make this a real procession and by happy coincidence a provocative act of witness as well. Join with other Christians in your town, and even if at a certain point you end up going in different directions to your different places of worship, this too at least bears witness to the scandalous disunity we too easily tolerate. And along with your palm crosses, wave actual branches and sing songs of joyful protest. For that first entry into Jerusalem was not a gentle Jesus demonstrating his humility by riding on a donkey, but a carefully executed and provocative plan: acting out the prophecy of Zechariah, Jesus makes his purposes plain. The Messiah is entering into his city. He is coming to the temple. He is bringing in a new order. It is not as those who sang 'Hosanna' expected. And very few will be able to follow all the way. But it was something that seized attention. Let us try to make our Palm Sunday processions do the same. Let them be signs of a new order.

The Palm Sunday liturgy also includes a reading of the Passion narrative, usually from the synoptic Gospel set for that year. Just like the overture in an opera, this reading maps the main themes of what will follow in the rest of the week, telling a story all at once that we are now going to unpick and tell in slow and painful detail through the other services of the week.

The services of Monday, Tuesday and Wednesday of Holy Week, whether they be Eucharistic or a simple office like Compline, should be thoughtful and meditative. They provide opportunity to reflect upon the other biblical stories of the week, not least the anointing at Bethany, a story that Scripture says will always be told 'wherever the good news is proclaimed' (Mark 14.9) but that is usually left out by the lectionaries; could that be because a woman is the hero? And lectionaries compiled by men? Surely not!

These services start to take us deeper into the unfolding story, and we should not rush to anticipate its conclusion. This is also a good time to walk the Stations of the Cross, another liturgy deserving of greater attention and use by all parts of the Church. After all, it is simply another telling of the story.

Then we come to what is known as the Triduum – the great three days of Maundy Thursday, Good Friday and the Vigil of Easter Eve or very early Easter morning. Each of these great liturgies deserves a chapter of its own, so forgive me for moving quite quickly over the details of what we offer. But with these services in particular it is even more important to see their unity.

Through the liturgical drama we travel with Jesus from the upper room where he washes his disciples' feet, to the table where he shares the Passover and breaks bread in an anticipation of his death, to the garden where he asks us to watch and pray with him, to the trial before Pilate, to the foot of the cross, to the barren darkness of the tomb, to the dawning brightness of the first Easter day. It is *one* celebration, stretched out over three days. It demands attention. It forces us to stop at each point along the way and see how we fit in. For this reason the honed liturgical ceremonial of the Triduum is our greatest ally, and in the Church today we urgently need to up our liturgical game, learn how to inhabit and present liturgical drama, and bring to these celebrations our best gifts of creativity and enterprise. So don't just read about Jesus washing people's feet, wash feet yourselves. And don't just wash one foot – whoever heard of such a mean-spirited offering? – wash them both. And why stop at the symbolic 12? Jesus washed all his disciples' feet, and had little patience for Peter when he tried to refuse the gift. So wash the feet of the whole congregation. I have seen it done a few times. Yes, it takes a while. Yes, it is deeply uncomfortable. But it looks and feels like the gospel.

There are also liturgies which enable you to celebrate the Eucharist of Maundy Thursday within the pattern of a Passover meal. This too brings out the significance of the meal: not just an act of fellowship, but even before Jesus gives it such new meaning, a meal redolent of salvation. Then make sure the service never quite finishes. No blessing. No dismissal. Just the invitation to stop and pray. So go from the table to a place of waiting. Re-create the Garden of Gethsemane in your church. Strip the rest of your church bare. Take down the crosses. Remove the ornaments. Take the sacrament from the aumbry, the cloths from the altars. Snuff out the candles. Take the water from the font. Experience what it is to be Church without church. To be one who follows Jesus without anything else. And when the time comes – for we all will leave at some point – find out what it is to be one who cannot watch and wait, who slips home and makes a cup of tea and catches up with what you've missed on television. Meanwhile Jesus goes to his death.

Many churches keep a watch of prayer till midnight and then read the Gospel of the arrest. Some go all through the night. And if we stay, we go home in the silence of the night or the first hours of morning and we are very aware that the service hasn't ended. We are pausing as Jesus undergoes the kangaroo court of a trial by night, and is himself awoken to be dragged before Herod and Pilate.

We too reconvene. The church building is still stripped naked. If possible this Good Friday service will be at those very hours that Jesus hung upon the cross, but of course today, with so many people constrained by work, sometimes it will have to be in the evening. But the liturgy still follows the story. The Passion narrative is read, this time from John. A cross is brought into the main body of the church. Often an invitation is sung by the priest three times: 'This is the wood of the cross on which our Redeemer hung. Come, come let us adore.' The congregation come forward.

I encourage people to come and gather round the cross as a crowd, not arrive one by one in an orderly English queue. Then, gathered around the cross, held by it, we sing a devotional song or hymn; and if people wish they come forward and kneel before the cross, and touch and hold it, or even bend low and kiss it. Indeed, some of my most precious memories of Holy Week are seeing very small children or those who are very tired and very old come forward in such a liturgy and simply kiss.

On Good Friday no Eucharist is celebrated. The bread that was consecrated on Maundy Thursday and reserved somewhere privately through the night is carried to the table. There is very little ceremonial. The Lord's Prayer is said. Holy Communion is received in silence. We go home.

Jesus is dead. The story is over. His body is taken from the cross and laid in the tomb. We are invited simply to grieve. Oh, blessed are those who mourn.

In many respects these services are, perhaps, the only ones each year that don't need a sermon. If the liturgy is conceived and celebrated in such a way that the story is told, then the liturgical drama *is* the sermon, *is* the breaking open of the word. And I say this as one who tends to preach at pretty much every service of the year, including the smallest gathering for a midweek Eucharist. But a way of deepening the experience of the Holy Week story is to punctuate these liturgies with other voices and other stories. So, for instance, I was once part of a church where different members of the congregation were invited to write different reflections as if they were different characters in the story. Then throughout the Triduum the action would, as it were, pause and people would step forward and speak in the first person as if the event had just taken place – which, in a sense, it had. So at the foot-washing Peter tells us why he feels things are the wrong way round and he should be washing Jesus' feet, not Jesus his. After Holy Communion Judas tells us why he is going off to betray Jesus. At the watch and at midnight those who fall asleep and those who cannot stay faithful tell us how they are feeling. At the cross Mary speaks from the sorrow of the sword that pierces her heart; and the centurion who nailed him there, rolled dice for his clothes and then declared him Son of God speaks about what it is to see this man die. And Joseph of Arimathea, a secret disciple – and, oh, there are still a good many of them around – explains why he asked Pilate for the body of Jesus. In fact one of the books I have written about the Passion story – *The Nail*[3] – began as a Good Friday meditation with several people taking different parts in the story and one by one justifying their actions and explaining why the death of Jesus could not be laid at their door.

The tradition of preaching the cross on Good Friday is very important for the Anglican tradition. Often the liturgy I have described above is presented as part of a traditional three-hour service of other readings and music. One of my other books, *The Things He Carried*,[4] began life as such a series of meditations which I preached in St Paul's Cathedral on Good Friday in 2005.

An extended Good Friday liturgy is a wonderful opportunity to imaginatively re-tell the story and get beneath its skin. It is a chance to be inventive and to use all the arts and all our creativity to tell the story.

In another church the Good Friday liturgy was punctuated by brief reflections from members of the congregation who brought their own experience to the story. So a nurse working in a local hospice spoke from the foot of the cross about her vocation to watch with those who are dying. A member of the armed forces spoke about the complexities and moral ambiguities of being one under orders, a bereaved person about bereavement. And if your main service on Good Friday is at the traditional time between noon and three, then there is also opportunity in the morning and the evening for other sorts of service. In Essex, where I now serve, the church in Maldon puts on a performance of Bach's *St John Passion* each Good Friday evening. But they do it liturgically, with brief prayers and with a sermon between the two acts of the piece. In the morning of Good Friday many churches have a children's liturgy, perhaps getting them to make and act the Stations of the Cross. It is also a day when many Christians from different churches get together for a public act of witness.

Fourth, Holy Week is a time to pay attention to what I think of as the silence between the notes. If Holy Week is this great liturgical drama, this opera in which we play and sing, then, as we know from other music, there are not just the notes on the page but the gaps between them. And with many beautiful and much loved pieces of music there is that experience where, as a phrase turns and unfolds, a melody resolves or twists in a new direction or an unexpected harmony jolts, a dissonance surprises, when you know what is coming next and you kind of long for it, but there is also that fraction of a second when the whole piece waits achingly for resolution. I have perhaps spent rather too much of my life listening to Chopin's *Nocturnes* and Mendelssohn's *Songs without Words*. I know them and I don't know them. They are familiar. And they are strange. And a slightly different interpretation of what I know so well releases the floodgates on new reservoirs of meaning and joy. And there is something about that expectant silence before the resolution of a phrase which is not only itself pregnant with meaning but renders the resolution even more joyful.

This is what Holy Week does. So play it slowly. Be open to new interpretations and the sound of other voices and other harmonies. Don't hurry it. And in the large spaces in between the liturgies when we go about our other business at home or at work, try to practise a mindfulness that keeps you walking with Jesus through the events of this week. Provide congregations with short prayers and readings that can be said in the home each day. Remind them that in the Christian faith you can only understand by *standing under*. This is the great mystery. Knowledge of God never comes pre-packaged. There is no handle on the cross. You cannot pick it up and carry it away. You have to stand there. You have to receive it.

On that first Good Friday, only a few people could do it. Those who promised most were first to flee. But let us be those who stand there today, not understanding but *standing under in order to understand*. Standing with empty hands and hopeful hearts. For it is only under the cross that we will begin to comprehend its meaning, receive its complicated joys and then help bear it to the world, not carrying it under our arm but shouldering it with Christ for the sake of the world. All this is the uncomfortable and beautiful gift of a good Holy Week.

And I want to tell you about Easter. I want to urge you to celebrate Easter late in the night or very early in the morning. I want to tell you about kindling a fire in the darkness; of dispelling the shadows of night; about a single light banishing darkness and then shared with swift and glorious luminosity to a gathered crowd of eager and surprised disciples. I want to urge you to read the Scriptures like a nomadic people gathered around a camp fire; I want to invite you to douse yourselves with holy water; to baptize and to confirm in the night; and to greet the dawn with a shout of defiant praise. But all that, I presume, is the subject of another chapter. So I leave you with the silence of Holy Saturday: the barren day, the day of waiting, the day of no celebration. Keep the flower arrangers out of the church for as long as possible. Cleaning brass and trimming wicks can wait a while. Of course we must make the church beautiful. But there is another beauty we have to enter into first: the beauty of the death of Christ, of his complete identification and sharing in what it is to be human, his lying in the cold stone of the tomb, his harrowing of hell, and the bewildered grief of those left behind. We need to share this: first, because we know it so well with the deaths, horrors and diminishments of our own living and loving, and the actual deaths of many loved ones, the many graves tended; but also because the resurrection must always be a shock and a surprise; the first piece of a new story, not the tagged-on happy ending of another. So attend; be bold; be imaginative; tread slowly; and have a very good Holy Week.

Notes

1 Edwin Muir, 'The killing', *Selected Poems*. London: Faber & Faber, 2008.
2 *Common Worship: Times and Seasons*. London: Church House Publishing, 2006.
3 *The Nail*. London: SPCK, 2011.
4 *The Things He Carried: A journey to the cross – meditations for Lent and Holy Week*. London: SPCK, 2008.

A good Easter

Stephen Conway
BISHOP OF ELY

In popular culture, any religious celebration of Easter appears in a minor key compared to Christmas; and yet we know that the Easter cycle is the season upon which all other seasons depend. The Lord who comes to share our life does so both with delight and with purpose: he shares our life in order to change it. We are invited to be transformed, even transfigured by resurrection life. The invitation issued to us, however we have received it, is to go deeper into an Easter faith. I used to work at Durham Cathedral. The Cathedral has at the west end a beautiful Galilee Chapel. The name signifies that it was the gathering place for processions through the Cathedral to the high altar at the east, symbolizing Jesus' journey from Galilee to Jerusalem and our journey from earth to heaven with him who has been raised from the dead.

In a recent Easter sermon on the last verses of St Mark's Gospel, I said:

The spine-tingling invitation is to follow Jesus by taking up our own cross, to lose our life for Jesus' sake in order to save it. The gospel is open-ended because we are invited to have faith that there is open space for us to inhabit in the new creation. There are the pages yet to be written of the gospel of Jesus Christ, the Son of

God, on your heart and mine. Fear and bewilderment are not the opposite of faith. Faith in God empowers us to dare to lose what is holding us back from finding our true worth in Christ. We can rest in not having all the answers. Happy endings which tie up all the loose ends are for fairy tales. Gospel endings are wide open with hope that Christ is risen. The open question is: will we follow him when he calls our name?

I want us to have this question in our minds as I ask us to reflect on four images.

David Wynne, Noli Me Tangere *(1963)*[1]

This sculpture anticipated the launch of Twiggy's modelling career by two years. To visitors in the 1960s, it must have looked both contemporary and strangely outside time.

Mary is struggling to recognize the figure in front of her, partly because he has been peeled back to skin and bone, more essence than person, and partly (if we interpret the hand shielding her eyes correctly) because of the light radiating from the resurrected Jesus. This Jesus would not pass for a gardener. His body is reminiscent of images of the crucified Christ and his hugely exaggerated bony hands would be of little use with a spade. They resemble the skeletal shape of wings as they point upwards, gesturing towards the ascension, but also enclosing him against physical contact. The artist has caught both Mary and Jesus in arrested motion. She walks towards him; he seems about to fly upwards. What anchors him? It occurs to me that he is anchored by love. This is the substance and the weight of the new creation.

In the build-up to this encounter, Mary Magdalene does not see this. She has seen the evidence that Jesus has risen, but has not felt the joy this might have prompted. The fact of the resurrection is cold and empty without the risen Lord right there. I have to confess that I have often preferred Good Friday to Easter Day. Friends tell me that I am an acute if smiling pessimist. As a would-be perfectionist, I often feel that I do not get beyond the dress rehearsal. It is not difficult to understand that some people never break free of the first fierceness of the wounds of bereavement and separation. I have known women in their 90s grieving the loss of a baby from over 70 years before. Mary represents that powerful pull of death. Outside the tomb, she is somehow outside the revelation of what has happened there. I don't know about you, but I have occasionally felt that I have been living outside myself. I think the Johannine contrast between flesh and spirit points to this: human sin and alienation puts us outside real life and what it might mean to abide in that fullness of life which Christ came to give us. Mary is surprised to meet angels rather than a corpse and turns away. The Greek phrase used, *eis ta opiso*, literally 'turning backwards', is used about those who rejected him as the Bread of Life in John 6.66.

Then Jesus does appear and she does not recognize him. The sculpture raises the question we would all love to ask: 'What was so different about Jesus' risen body that people who knew him well didn't recognize him?' The experience of non-recognition is not, in itself, so foreign. We have all met people we know in the 'wrong' context and failed to acknowledge them: the archdeacon in running attire for his marathon training, the supermarket cashier you always talk to who is in the same queue at the cinema. It's also not uncommon for the recently bereaved to think they see the deceased sitting in a favourite chair or disappearing round a corner. Family members who have been away for a time and return enormously changed by illness or by sudden ageing may be met with blank stares on the doorstep. None of these scenarios quite seems to fit. Jesus has only been away three days and Mary has gone to find him in the place where he should have been.

The resurrection changes the way everything is seen. It is even conceivable that it makes us visible to God in a new way. The Proper Preface for Easter (adapted from the Ambrosian Rite – the second Wednesday of Easter) puts it this way:

> It is indeed right, our duty and our joy,
> always and everywhere to give you thanks . . .
> For by the mystery of his passion
> Jesus Christ, your risen Son,
> has conquered the powers of death and hell
> and restored in men and women the image of your
> glory.[2]

Mary is the first redeemed human being Jesus sees. There must be something in this of the wonder of the first creation (Genesis 1.26–31), so it is not surprising that poets and iconographers have played with the idea that 'Christ's cross and Adam's tree stood in one place' (John Donne, 'A hymn to God my God, in my sickness'). This 'Sonnet for Easter dawn' by Malcolm Guite is a meditation on the meeting the sculpture describes, adding as its original touch that the

Word which makes us live might be our own name in the mouth of God:

XV Easter dawn

He blesses every love which weeps and grieves
And now he blesses hers who stood and wept
And would not be consoled, or leave her love's
Last touching place, but watched as low light crept
Up from the east. A sound behind her stirs
A scatter of bright birdsong through the air.
She turns, but cannot focus through her tears,
Or recognise the Gardener standing there.
She hardly hears his gentle question 'Why,
Why are you weeping?', or sees the play of light
That brightens as she chokes out her reply
'They took my love away, my day is night'
And then she hears her name, she hears Love say
The Word that turns her night, and ours, to Day.[3]

Following Mary Magdalene as our representative, living the resurrection means that the consequence of being seen and named by the risen Christ is that we are invited to see what being invited to be a new creation might mean. The world is turned the right way up because a woman can be a witness just like a man and has the freedom, just like a man, not to see. Some say that Mary Magdalene is the representative of the unseeing people of Israel, waiting to catch up with the recognition of the Christ as the long-expected Messiah. She certainly represents us in our modern living, catching up in our imagination and in the music of our praise with new life. Whatever living the resurrection might mean for

you and me, it is about every bit of you and me. There is
no life now without resurrection as its spring. The transfiguring power of love is at work in us. We may not feel it
always in our weakness and distraction, but we have been
given treasure:

> But we have this treasure in clay jars, so that it may
> be made clear that this extraordinary power belongs to
> God and does not come from us. We are afflicted in
> every way, but not crushed; perplexed, but not driven
> to despair; persecuted, but not forsaken; struck down,
> but not destroyed; always carrying in the body the
> death of Jesus, so that the life of Jesus may also be made
> visible in our bodies. (2 Corinthians 4.7–10)

Piero della Francesca, The Resurrection *(1463–5)*[4]

Piero painted this resurrection scene for the Council Hall
of Borgo di Sansepolcro in the province of Arezzo in
Tuscany. The town seems to have taken its name from the
relics brought back by two citizens who had been to the
Holy Land (Sansepolcro means 'holy sepulchre') and early
chroniclers referred to it as 'the New Jerusalem'. Was this
in the artist's mind when he painted Christ emerging
from the tomb? Certainly, during the Second World War,
a British artillery officer called Tony Clarke defied orders to
shell Sansepolcro because he had read Aldous Huxley's essay,
'The best picture' (1925) and could not imagine destroying
something so important.

There are several things to note about the scene. The tomb
itself is a classical sarcophagus, alluding to antiquity and

to a pre-Christian past. The emerging figure is entirely unlike the emaciated body depicted by David Wynne. This Christ is muscular and athletic. His posture and the drape of his robe have an imperial character. Yet there is something at first sight ludicrous about placing this majestic Christ in relation to the rest of the picture. Behind him is a rustic hillside scene, perhaps drawing on the local landscape. The sleeping guards in the foreground are in the clothing of the artist's period. They are sleeping through the final conquest of death, and we might feel that, were they to wake up, they would join the many who did not recognize the risen Jesus because of the limitations of their own expectations. He turns up in the wrong place, or in the wrong shape or clothing. The severely injured corpse they had been set to watch is only faintly alluded to in the small scar on Jesus' right side. Otherwise, he is Christ in Majesty, at the same time statuesque and poised for action. He carries a banner of victory, and his crown may be made of thorns but it looks like the golden coronet of an emperor. This is a picture of nobility and strength, which Huxley – unsurprisingly – says has very little to do with its Christian theme. He sees it as the best picture in the world because of what it has to say about the human spirit. However, I am intrigued and inspired by the representation of that perfect union of the abiding and beautiful human character of the resurrection with the divine vindication and power of the God who glorifies the beauty revealed on the cross and the grace that flows to all creation from that place.

There is no place or situation where the risen Christ does not have access. In the Alan Bennett sermon, 'there is always a bit in the corner of the sardine tin that one can't get out. Is there a little bit in the corner of your life? I know there is in mine.' In Psalm 139 we meet the inescapable God:

> Where can I go from your spirit?
>> Or where can I flee from your presence?
> If I ascend to heaven, you are there;
>> if I make my bed in Sheol, you are there.
> If I take the wings of the morning
>> and settle at the farthest limits of the sea,
> even there your hand shall lead me,
>> and your right hand shall hold me fast.
> If I say, 'Surely the darkness shall cover me,
>> and the light around me become night',
> even the darkness is not dark to you;
>> the night is as bright as the day,
>> for darkness is as light to you.
>
> (verses 7–12)

The risen Christ who bursts from the tomb is the one who has first descended to the depths before he ascends on high. The prologue of John's Gospel is wholly fulfilled: 'The light shines in the darkness, and the darkness did not overcome it.'

Living in a post-Christendom culture, such an image of Christ as the noblest expression of the classical ideal can appear passé and arrogant. Nevertheless, we are reminded that the inescapable God is the source of all creativity and liberty of thought and imagination. The risen Christ reigns in the architecture of all our learning and reflection. As those living Easter, we are light-bearers and those who are called to open up spaces with and for others. We must not lose our courage – particularly in our capital city – to promote and live the new creation in the abundance of our ideas and hopes which we desire to bring to bear on the shaping of the city. What starts here has the opportunity to inform the world. The world may sleep, but Christ still emerges unexpectedly over our barricades to bring about the profound revolution of the kingdom, bearing the banner of love. The apparently ludicrous revelation of Christ in the regional landscape painted by Piero is no accident. We are given the power and responsibility to be looking for and building Easter environments for people. Earlier today I met with a property developer who understood my ambition to enable people to live where they sleep, to be parts of communities, not dormitories within the civic landscape.

Stanley Spencer, The Resurrection with the Raising of Jairus's Daughter[5]

Resurrection had been a theme in Spencer's painting following the end of the First World War and the resurrection theme continued to occupy him as the Second World War ended. He had been working as a war artist at Port Stanley, near Glasgow, and one day he walked up a hill where there was a cemetery. He recorded that this reminded him of the Hill of Sion, and he began work on a series of large panels, using local people (shipyard workers and their families) as his inspiration. Out of this came eight very large canvases. Three of them make up the triptych (now in Southampton) of *The Resurrection with the Raising of Jairus's Daughter*, completed around 1947.

Reproductions fail to convey the detail and animation of this painting. In the centre panel is the scene in Jairus' house, an ordinary, small, unpretentious red-brick building of the period. Through the window, we see the little girl sitting up on a bed. Jesus stands at the foot of the bed, pointing to heaven. Other bystanders, overcome with emotion, bury their faces in their hands.

Outside the doorway of the house, in the left-hand panel, the wonder that has just occurred is linked to a scene of wild rejoicing and reunion by women emerging on to the pavement from the house. Perhaps they have come out to report the child's healing. Over one of the external doors is a small Union Jack. It seems slightly frivolous – the sort of thing that would be suitable for a street party celebrating victory. It is a quirky and domestic reminder of the flag of victory in the hand of Piero's Christ. The pavement itself is erupting as people emerge from under its slabs. We must assume that they are the dead being raised, helped out by each other and by the living.

A figure leaning out of a bedroom window in the right-hand panel links the central events to another set of reunions, this time apparently between mothers and children. The dominant note is one of joy. There is no reticence or estrangement or lack of recognition.

What do we make of Jesus' finger pointing upwards? Spencer was interested in heaven, and his paintings of resurrection scenes suggest that he thought of it as a place of re-creation, where people were themselves made new and filled with happiness, whatever they had been through in the past. Is

94

Jesus suggesting that heaven is all around, that the animated goings on outside are not a distraction but a breaking in of heaven on earth?

The Lucan account of the miracle of the raising of Jairus' daughter (Luke 8.40–56) is set in an interesting sequence of events. He has gone into Samaria with some of his disciples and also some women, including one whom he had healed of demonic possession. He tells them parables on the way: the story of the sower and of the lamp hidden under an upturned vessel. Then he encounters the Gerasene demoniac (we still struggle to find the language for the severely mentally ill people whose torment did not frighten and repel Jesus the way it did others) and heals him. And then he is summoned urgently to the house of Jairus, on the way healing another social outcast, the woman with the haemorrhage. By the time he gets to Jairus' house, there is ample evidence of his power over sickness in all its forms, his power to transform the way people are seen by their nearest companions. Now he is challenged to raise the dead, and in the face of the ridicule of official mourners and bystanders he does this, focusing on the faith of the child's parents. We are not told whether any of those healed were among the 72 sent out to take the message of the kingdom further (Luke 10). If they were, then Spencer's vivid imagery helps us to imagine the authentic joy of first-hand experience with which they carried their news. This chimes so closely with Rowan Williams' thesis that the resurrection is first an experience of forgiveness and healing which creates new patterns of life together and so reveals a fresh understanding of a social God, not tied to God's physical presence but to the identity of the community in the power of God's Spirit.

Peter Eugene Ball, Christus Rex[6]

This was a millennium commission for Ely Cathedral. It is mounted on a pillar behind the pulpit and has the extra-ordinary effect of hovering over the preacher. With their elongated faces and huge eyes, Ball's characteristic gilded driftwood figures are not unlike Romanesque depictions of Christ in Majesty. That is in keeping with the Cathedral, which was begun in its present form in 1083.

Often these figures have the index and middle finger raised, as in the Ely *Christus Rex,* and one might conclude quickly that this was a gesture of blessing. There is another possibil-ity, however. In the system of formal hand gestures that was part of classical rhetoric, this can be an instruction to keep silent. There is good reason for this in depictions of Christ. When he appears in judgement, he is the one who speaks and others must be quiet. If you see him with the evangelists, their scrolls are rolled up and their books closed. There is no further call for them to talk about Jesus because he is risen and his word is eternal. With that in mind, it is a difficult challenge to be a preacher in Ely.

This particular image of Christ may be a judge, but the facial expression suggests that he is a benign judge. This is the God whose judgement is to have mercy, who came that we might have life in abundance, whatever the cost to him. This is he who was raised up in order to draw all people to himself. Jean Vanier was recently asked whether he had any further reflection on his study of St John's Gospel. He observed that the true majesty of Christ was revealed when he established the future community of the gospel in the persons of his friend and his mother at the point of his greatest humiliation and disability. This is his lived parable of judgement on Boko Haram and all our blasphemies of violence and greed.

Between the ascension and the second coming with its time of judgement is the space in which the Church is called to live. Luke goes on: 'And they worshipped him, and returned to Jerusalem with great joy; and they were continually in the temple blessing God' (Luke 24.52–53).

We are called to the same joy; but we cannot ignore the fact that joy is always imperfect, fragile and threatened. By a strange paradox, the consciousness of that which, beyond all passing pleasure, would constitute true happiness also includes the certainty that there is no perfect happiness. The experience of finiteness, felt by each generation in its turn, obliges one to acknowledge and to plumb the immense gap that always exists between reality and the desire for the infinite.

This paradox and this difficulty in attaining joy seem to us particularly acute today. This is the reason for our message. Technological society has succeeded in multiplying the opportunities for pleasure, but it has great difficulty in generating joy. For joy comes from another source. It is the joy of living Easter.

I bought a tile, as a resting place for a hot dish, on which was written 'Alleluia anyway!' and I am much taken by the statue of Mary Magdalene by Donatello which was carved in 1453 for the Duomo in Florence. It is far from other

Renaissance representations of Mary as a courtesan. It is a penitent Mary, leading a life of reparation, conflated with the Eastern Church's traditions of St Margaret of Egypt. Donatello was by now in his 60s and was beginning to produce works which were studies in ageing. He was fascinated by the figure of John the Baptist as well as Mary Magdalene. Look her up on your smartphones and you can see the older Mary. She still bears the marks of the one freed from terrible mental anguish. You can hardly tell where her wild hair ends and her rags begin. But she is on the front foot. She is framed as a witness to Easter faith. Mary Magdalene discovered that she need no longer be defined as a person by her sins or by other people's categories of what constitutes acceptable mental health. She has accepted the restoration of the inner beauty that is the birthright of the sons and daughters of God. When this statue went for restoration some years ago, the restorers discovered that Donatello had threaded her hair with gold leaf.

I am unlikely to be so bedecked, but the principle is to be lived. A good Easter is life lived shot through with grace and glory, hoping for that transfiguring by love which makes us the healed and forgiven community of the resurrection.

Notes

1 See <https://www.flickr.com/photos/16162181@N05/14182690817>.
2 *Common Worship: Times and Seasons*. London: Church House Publishing, 2006, p. 437.
3 From *Sounding the Seasons*. Norwich: Canterbury Press, 2012.

4 See <https://www.khanacademy.org/humanities/renaissance-reformation/early-renaissance1/central-italy1/a/piero-della-francesca-resurrection>.

5 See <http://www.royal-painting.com/largeimg/Stanley%20Spencer/48304-Stanley%20Spencer--Unknown.jpg>.

6 See <http://www.petereball.com/wp-content/gallery/religious/christus-rex-ely-1999.jpg>.

A good Pentecost

Karen Gorham
BISHOP OF SHERBORNE

The story is told of a little boy who, on coming home from Sunday School, told his mum that the vicar had said that God was everywhere. 'That is true,' his mother responded. 'Is he in the oven when it's hot?' the boy asked. 'Yes,' replied the mother. 'How about in the cupboard?' 'Yes,' said the mother. 'How about the fridge when the door is closed and the light is off?' 'Oh, yes,' retorted the mother. 'How about the cake tin?' asked the boy, as he took the lid off the tin. 'Well, I suppose he is,' answered the mother. The boy slammed the tin shut and announced triumphantly, 'Got him!' Of course, the mother had a lot more explaining to do!

As humorous as this story may be, there is some truth in it. Often we can view God in ways similar to this boy – we can think that God is small enough for us to put into a tidy package, which we are able to control and understand completely. We want God of our own making, on our own terms, a domesticated, tame God, and rather than accepting the fact that we humans are created in God's image, we can want to create a god in our version of the human image.

At the festival of Pentecost the Church is marking the first outpouring of the Spirit, described by Luke in Acts 2; on that day God could not be contained. The disciples, who had been hiding behind locked doors in fear following the resurrection and then waiting after the ascension as Christ commanded them to do, were driven out and, as people watched and listened to them, the word of God was propelled from their lips in languages all could understand. The Holy Spirit came upon them and they ventured forth into the world, God among them and among us, within, for ever. The Church that day was born and that same dynamism, the creative activity of God which was there at the beginning of time and which empowered Jesus, was now present in the Church.

Waiting

A good Pentecost begins with the waiting, something we all dislike doing when faced with the temptation of instant results and action. It is as if our perspective needs to change to enable God's strength to work in us, rather than us to work in our own strength.

The disciples had been instructed to wait in Jerusalem for the promised gift of the Holy Spirit. They were dependent upon Christ's promise. St John's Gospel reveals more about this for us, as John includes many references to the Spirit in Jesus' farewell discourses. As the Father sent the Son into the world as his representative, so the Spirit will be sent in Jesus' name (5.43, 14.26); just as Jesus taught the truth, so the Spirit of truth will lead them into all truth (14.6, 17, 15.26); just as Jesus remained with and guided the disciples, so will the Spirit (14.16–18); Jesus bore witness to the Father, and the Spirit will bear witness to Jesus (15.26–27).

The resurrection was a source of hope for them, but also raised in them that question of fulfilment – when, O Lord ... when would the kingdom of God come? This waiting is not to be empty: instead, the disciples wait in that hope; they now know that their Lord has been exalted, and they have been witnesses. There is a job to be done and they will be given power to do it.

So the disciples gather to pray, not always seen as the most 'useful' activity, yet the effort called for is greater than any strenuous action. This is to be a gift given in God's own time, not through endless activity and human striving.

This is anticipated in the Old Testament as we are given quite vivid images of individuals being called by God to wait; it is reflected, for example, in Isaiah 40.31 where we learn that two primary activities of the people of God are gathering to wait and pray: 'but those who wait for the LORD shall renew their strength, they shall mount up with wings like eagles, they shall run and not be weary, they shall walk and not faint'. Karl Barth described this time between Ascension and Pentecost as a 'significant pause' between the mighty acts of God, a pause in which the Church is invited to wait and pray for the coming of the Spirit, *veni Sancte Spiritus* ...

The coming of the Spirit at Pentecost prompts our own waiting. We wait today because we cannot do everything in our own strength; our dependence on Almighty God is such that we are powerless without God. Divine empowerment is needed, which we cannot earn or purchase but have to receive as a God-given gift.

In one of my former parishes we had come to a period in our church life when we felt we had lost our direction. New energy and vision was required. There were countless activities going on, filling people's time and deploying their talents, but these had created a busyness which left little space for God's word or God's Spirit to come in a new way. So we decided to stop all our activities from January until Easter and instead to meet and to pray together weekly. It involved a great deal of discipline, and much disappointment for those for whom the routine activities had become their life. However, it allowed space to pray as a church and, more importantly, to listen to what God was saying. We held a night of prayer and people were invited to share verses of Scripture or thoughts that they had had in their personal prayer times.

Now, I have nothing startling to report at the end of our time. We did not experience revival, but our spiritual growth as individuals and as a church was deepened as a result. We much more carefully and intentionally put events and activities back together again, and worn-out individuals were refreshed and renewed as others discovered longings and gifts which had lain dormant. Vocations were discerned and the church's soul was re-energized, so much so that I would always recommend considering a stopping and waiting time periodically in the local church.

I often wonder what those disciples did as they waited. The Bible gives us some clues. First, they prepared themselves practically. We read that the community that gathered included the women who had been with Jesus since Galilee as well as Jesus' mother and brothers – barriers were being broken down. It was also very much a Jewish community. The fact that there were 120 meant that they had enough men to form a synagogue with its own council, indicating that already there were enough people to form a legitimate community. And one of the immediate tasks for the new community, following the betrayal and death of Judas, was to pray for new leadership, and then to appoint another disciple who had been with, and was a witness to, Jesus. Matthias becomes one of the Twelve, chosen by God from among them.

Second, those who gathered reflected together on the words that Jesus had spoken to them about the coming of the Spirit. No doubt what they had been told would have informed their prayers. Jesus had promised that the heavenly Father would give the Spirit to those who asked him (Luke 11.9–13).

Several Old Testament passages refer to the continuing function of the Spirit in the creation and sustaining of life, beginning with the passage in Genesis 1.1–2, when the wind of the Spirit swept over the face of the waters at the beginning of creation, and in Genesis 2.7, when the Lord God formed Adam from the dust in the ground and breathed into him the breath of life so he became a living being. John the Baptist said that, while he was baptizing with water, Jesus would baptize with the Holy Spirit and fire (Luke 3.16). The apostles would have been witnesses to the Spirit descending upon Jesus at his baptism, and after his resurrection Christ himself breathed the Spirit upon them in a way resonant of Genesis 2.

Those who waited may well have recalled that time when Jesus, after being filled with the Spirit at his baptism, stood up in the synagogue, unfurled the scroll and read from the prophet Isaiah those words which established his ministry:

> The Spirit of the Lord is upon me,
>   because he has anointed me
>   to bring good news to the poor.
> He has sent me to proclaim release to the captives
>   and recovery of sight to the blind,
>   to let the oppressed go free,
> to proclaim the year of the Lord's favour.
>
> (Luke 4.18–19)

Is that what they too were to do? There would surely have been much anticipation as they waited for the fulfilment of Jesus' promised gift of the Holy Spirit to them.

The day of Pentecost

And so the scene is set. The story of Pentecost is a story to which the faith community returns again and again as its guide to life. While many interpretations can be offered for what happened in that upper room, we need to take events at face value. What happened is miraculous, supernatural and beyond the bounds of imagination, the only way to explain what drove the disciples out and gave them courage to proclaim the truth about Jesus Christ.

That same mystery is present still today: the Spirit that is God moves where he (or she) chooses, we often cannot understand it but so often can see the result of his or her presence. As Jesus said to Nicodemus (John 3.8), 'The wind blows where it chooses, and you hear the sound of it, but you do not know where it comes from or where it goes.'

It is dawn, and the day of Pentecost begins with the sound of wind and of heaven. Things are breaking open, coming loose. Can it be that creation wind again?

What is first heard is then seen: tongues like fire (Acts 2.3) come upon the disciples, the fulfilment of John the Baptist's prophecy. Tongues of fire turn into 'other tongues' as the Spirit gives utterance, and the new community moves out into the world. A crowd is gathering, devout Jews of every nation in Jerusalem for the festival, who are naturally per- plexed at all they are witnessing. The language is of every nation under heaven, as all hear in their own tongue.

'What does this mean?' is an obvious question when con- fronted by the God of power and the God of mystery. Who among us has not asked it when we see things we do not understand, have never seen before or whose meaning is hidden from our eyes? We, like those onlookers at Pentecost, try to rationalize God, search for plausible explanations. 'They must be drunk.' The in-breaking of the Spirit is pro- foundly unsettling and sometimes threatening, now as then.

In the second chapter of Acts, Luke describes the beginning of the rest of the story, which continues through the book of Acts and beyond. The Church's proclamation throughout the centuries always encounters enquiring minds, which provoke our storytelling as well as sometimes reducing us to silence. Thus the Spirit's role is needed in giving each of us voice, and helping us speak of the faith we hold, 'which faith the

Church is called upon to proclaim afresh in each generation', words from the Declaration of Assent which Anglican clergy and licensed lay ministers make on taking up a new appointment.

In Genesis the Spirit of God breathed life into dust and created a human being. In Acts the Spirit of God breathed life into the new Christian community and goes on doing so, bringing renewal to minds, refreshment to bodies and an overwhelming desire to praise God and witness to God in the world.

St Paul informs our understanding as he instructs the early church into the ways of the Spirit, helping Christians to proclaim and pray, serve and grow. We trust the Spirit's presence and, by waiting and praying, remain amazed at the God of surprises.

And so in a sense, the one day of Pentecost prepares Christians for a lifetime. As we grow in our faith from baptism onwards, we are not only reminded of God's power at work then but of the availability of God's power with us now, equipping us, calling us, comforting us, giving us gifts, enabling us to do things we never thought possible.

The Spirit in the Church

Church history also gives witness to times when Christians have been reawakened by the Spirit's power. It is not always easy to see why such revivals of praise, renewal and proclamation have occurred, but such events have contributed to the growth and witness of the Church across the world. In significant ways huge revivals in the early twentieth century prepared the way for the birth of Pentecostalism and subsequent 'outpourings' of the Spirit, and in smaller ways renewal has led individuals to become important witnesses for Christ in challenging and alien contexts.

Given our desire to package God and the impossibility of doing so, it is unsurprising that Christians have not always shared the same understanding of the work of the Holy Spirit. Before the emergence of the holiness movement in the mid-nineteenth century and Pentecostalism in the early twentieth century, most denominations believed that Christians received the baptism of the Holy Spirit either upon conversion or through the rites of Christian initiation. At the Reformation Zwingli spoke of a three-fold baptism – water, teaching and the Spirit: baptism and confirmation have both had their part to play.

Renewal and revival movements, however, have derived from Scripture the understanding that there should be prayer for the Spirit to come into an individual's life, accompanied by spiritual gifts including speaking in tongues. Thus the baptism of the Spirit has been seen as a distinct experience, a second work of grace, that empowers a person for Christian life and service.

In the book of Acts, when Peter and John were sent from Jerusalem to Samaria, we learn that although the new believers had been baptized with water, the Holy Spirit had not yet fallen on them; the Spirit instead was received by the laying on of hands (Acts 8). Later in Acts, when Peter preached the gospel to the household of Cornelius, the Holy Spirit fell on the Gentiles while he was speaking and they were subsequently baptized (Acts 10). The practice of prayer with the laying on of hands to impart the gift of the Holy Spirit, as something separate from baptism, can therefore be seen in the early church, and this was the origin of the sacrament of confirmation, the Western church separating the two rites from one another.

After his conversion in 1821, Presbyterian minister and revivalist Charles Finney experienced what he called 'baptism in the Holy Spirit' accompanied by 'unutterable gushings' of praise. He and others agreed that this was a life-altering experience subsequent to conversion, part of a continuing process enabling believers to give themselves to Christ's service.

Charismatic Christians trace their origins to the charismatic movement of the 1960s and 1970s. Unlike the Pentecostals, there are differing viewpoints on whether Spirit baptism is subsequent to conversion and whether speaking in tongues is always a sign of receiving the baptism. The emphasis has become more on empowerment than on salvation. Thus the courage of individuals such as Jackie Pullinger, who in 1966 went by boat to Hong Kong and subsequently developed an extraordinarily fruitful ministry to drug addicts and street sleepers there, is understood to be due to the work of the Holy Spirit enabling people to go where God leads, reliant on God's gifts to bring about the proclamation of the gospel and bring blessing to others.

Anglicans continue to hold differing views of the work of the Holy Spirit in the Church today and many of us cannot be pinned down to any one view, nor would wish to be.

Many clergy understand the gift of the Holy Spirit to be given in the sacraments of baptism and confirmation, as well as recognizing the importance of praying for an empowering of God the Spirit at other times. Many of us, through the influence of the charismatic movement including the ministry of John Wimber, David Pytches and New Wine, can testify to having experienced the power of the Spirit in our own lives through prayer and God working in ways we do not find easy to describe, let alone understand. The Anglican renewal movement of the 1980s stirred up in many a new desire to serve Christ resulting in a growth then in those going forward for ordination, a renewal of the Church's worship and healing ministry, and the development of new initiatives such as Alpha, which particularly emphasizes the work of the Holy Spirit in discipleship.

Our continuing tradition of infant baptism makes it necessary in our practice and liturgy to provide an opportunity for adults to make a public commitment of faith and to receive prayer for empowerment to live the Christian life. Confirmation, now more a choice than undertaken as a matter of course, can do just that as it offers an opportunity for testimony to be shared and a period of waiting and prayer for the Holy Spirit to empower and confirm a person for Christian discipleship, and ends with sending the newly confirmed out into the world.

There is also a need to reinvigorate the life of the local Church by offering continuing opportunities for individuals to be recommissioned and the Church to be renewed for the task of conveying the good news of the gospel to the world. Many churches, particularly in the charismatic tradition, now offer regular prayer for healing and empowering alongside the receiving of bread and wine on a Sunday, and prayer for the guidance of the Holy Spirit is a regular occurrence before many church meetings or events.

In many churches and towns the celebration of Pentecost itself has become a time for coming together as Christians and praying afresh for this empowerment by God's Spirit, for the renewal of particular places, for healing, and for church and individual growth.

Empowered for service

Christ taught that as Christians we are expected to bear fruit, and this fruitfulness is the sign that any Christian is filled with the Spirit, whether through baptism, confirmation or empowering prayer. The gift of the Holy Spirit is never for personal gain or glory, but always for the blessing of others. Hence the emphasis St Paul placed on the fruits of the Spirit as well as the gifts, and on practical gifts as well as spiritual (and inward) ones. The story of the Spirit's descent at Pentecost was never about something purely personal. Luke's narrative about fire and wind, language and proclamation, tells us that something of ultimate importance is happening. The Spirit of God is unleashed, bringing confusion for some, empowerment to others and a breath of hope to the waiting and listening world.

We all know the adage that a Christian can be so heavenly minded as to be of no earthly use, thus emphasizing that always we need to ask for God's grace to enable us to be the people God wants us to be in a spirit of service and vocation. The journey of the Church beginning at Pentecost is a vocational one: it is the story of the people of the Way of Jesus Christ. The Holy Spirit in our daily life should cause us to always follow our Lord and Saviour, using the gifts that he has given us. A good Pentecost is about establishing a pattern to live by, as well as seeing our life as a journey or pilgrimage which brings us encounters, challenges and opportunities that, equipped by the Spirit of God, we can rise to. It is therefore appropriate that, when an individual makes a decision to follow Christ's call on his or her life which is then affirmed by the Church through the laying on of hands, the liturgy includes a significant acknowledgement of the empowering work of the Spirit of God through prayer and the invocation of the Holy Spirit.

The hymn 'Veni Creator Spiritus' ('Come, Creator Spirit') is believed to have been written by Rabanus Maurus in the ninth century. As an invocation of the Holy Spirit, in the Roman Catholic Church it is sung during the liturgical celebration of Pentecost. In the Anglican Church, after appearing in the Ordaining of Priests and the Consecration of Bishops in the 1662 Book of Common Prayer, it has become part of our formal liturgy. It is used not only for ordinations and consecrations, but also importantly since the coronation of King Charles I in 1625 in every coronation as the sovereign is dressed in a white alb and seated in the coronation chair prior to being anointed.

> Come, Holy Ghost, our souls inspire,
> And lighten with celestial fire.
> Thou the anointing Spirit art,
> Who dost thy sevenfold gifts impart.

The sevenfold gifts refer to Isaiah 11.2 and are wisdom, understanding, counsel, fortitude, knowledge, piety and the fear of the Lord. The imparting of these gifts of the Spirit comes as the gathered community together waits and prays for those being baptized, confirmed, ordained or crowned, in recognition of the need for the special anointing power of the Holy Spirit because no one can respond to God's call and serve God in their own strength alone.

Pentecost, however, shows that God the Holy Spirit is not just for a chosen few, but a gift for every baptized believer to enable the whole Church to do what it was called to do. As I license clergy to a new ministry, often in a new place with new people, I try to reaffirm that joint calling of priest and people together. One message I have repeated is the encouragement for each person to be the person God called him or her to be. None of us can pretend we are someone else, and the gospel can only be attractive to others through our own integrity and authenticity. However, being the person God calls us to be is not static, it is ever evolving, and so together Christian communities are called to become more Christ-like: to live out through love and service what it means to be Christians in that place, not for its own sake but to bring blessing there.

Pentecost can, if we are not careful, be the Church's annual birthday party to the exclusion of everyone outside. I, along with I expect a good number of clergy, have cajoled the congregation into turning up to the Sunday service dressed in red! Yet it stands in our calendar to remind us that it marks the beginning of the rest of our lives, and it is for the sake of those outside it that the Spirit came in the first place. We need to return again and again to those words quoted by Jesus from the prophet Isaiah and be reminded that we are to be transformers of a needy world, and people who get their hands dirty, as well as witnesses to God's word.

As a child I used to go to Sunday School in the church hall while my parents attended the main church service. One day Sunday School finished early and I arrived at the church door at the same time as the vicar appeared through it to greet the congregation as they went home. 'Has the service finished?' I eagerly asked. 'Church has finished,' said my wise vicar, 'but the service now begins!' You can see I have not forgotten his words!

As a bishop one of the joys of my ministry is confirmation. It is a rite of the Church which has come in for a fair amount of criticism over the years and has caused many to consider its purpose and meaning. Confirmation has been seen as far removed from the lively Sunday worship experienced in our larger churches, and when a growing number of adult converts have not been baptized confirmation can seem to be an unnecessary add-on. However, a reflection on the work of God's Holy Spirit and the feast of Pentecost can help us see the importance of having a corporate celebration of individual commitment where the Christian community gathers to testify to the work of God in lives today. It is a sign of unity which signifies that Christians belong to the universal Church and an act of witness to those who do not yet know God.

Private preparation for public witness

Confirmation is both a public and a private occasion: commitments are made inwardly and promises spoken outwardly, reflecting that pattern at Pentecost as the followers of Jesus began to form the community we now call the Church. Public events are important because they are just that – public. On display. Other people are watching, watching not only the event itself but also for people's reactions to it. Life out in public needs careful thought and preparation. People will judge Christianity through the followers of Christ, by our own public behaviour.

We can see in the pattern of Jesus' own life the importance of both the public and the private, particularly in teaching the disciples how they should use the times away from the public gaze to pray and be renewed. Christ himself set aside time to pray in between speaking to the crowds.

Jesus would often meet with his closest disciples, and we often find them gathering around a table for a meal. It is during those times, in private, that their leader – their teacher, their Lord – tells his followers how thankful he is for them, expresses confidence that they will be faithful in doing the work he has given them and lets them know how eager he is for all of them to be together again. They share bread, wine, conversation and friendship. And as this small group spends quiet, private time together, they are strengthened, encouraged and renewed for their next appearance in public – beyond the crucifixion, resurrection and ascension – for service in the world.

On the feast of Pentecost, the disciples went public! And like those first disciples, through us the world will come to know God. This means that we are an important part of God's plan of love and salvation, and so it is with us too that during these private times we learn to be the bearers of God's good news through Jesus Christ.

Confirmation is also about the private bit being everything we do in church, preparing us for the public bit when we get outside, what we do when we leave; it establishes a pattern for our Christian living.

In those quieter, private times, Jesus calls us – his close friends – to be with him at table. Jesus invites us to share bread and wine and conversation, and as we Christians come together regularly, Jesus encourages us, just as he did his first disciples, in our ability to do the work he has given us, that we will go forth into the world and do that work faithfully and well. We do not do that in our own strength but through the power of the Holy Spirit, that same power that came at Pentecost; and so we pray for the Spirit's power.

The message I find myself telling confirmation candidates is that we can be encouraged because that group who were sent out that day full of the Holy Spirit was relatively small. And if that small group was given what was needed then to start the Church, what potential there is for those of us who are Christians today to bring change for good in the world, and to bring about transformation by our words and actions as we ourselves are being transformed. At that first Pentecost God's love overflowed the disciples to the point where they were able to make the message of Jesus' love understood by everyone. It was credible because they let God's glory, and not their own, shine through.

Easter, Ascension and Pentecost are intrinsically linked. The liturgy of Pentecost marks the culmination of the great 50-day celebration of the resurrection.

The time between Pentecost and the coming of the kingdom of God in all its fullness is where we now find ourselves; it is the in-between time of witness, and Pentecost reveals the power we present-day disciples need to continue to fulfil our calling to make Christ known.

The ascension as described by Luke ends with the question to the disciples: 'Why do you stand looking up towards heaven?' (Acts 1.11). There is work for us to do. Therefore the liturgical season ends appropriately with Pentecost leading us into ordinary time, and so the ordinary can be made extraordinary each and every day by the Spirit of God as we are commissioned to 'Go in peace to love and serve the Lord in the name of Christ.' Amen to that.

Copyright acknowledgements

Did you know that SPCK is a registered charity?

As well as publishing great books by leading Christian authors, we also . . .

. . . make assemblies meaningful and fun for over a million children by running www.assemblies.org.uk, a popular website that provides free assembly scripts for teachers. For many children, school assembly is the only contact they have with Christian faith and culture, and the only time in their week for spiritual reflection.

. . . help prisoners to become confident readers with our easy-to-read stories. Poor literacy is a huge barrier to rehabilitation. Prisoners identify with the believable heroes of our gritty fiction. At the same time, questions at the end of each chapter help them to examine their choices from a moral perspective and to build their reading confidence.

. . . support student ministers overseas in their training through partnerships in the Global South.

Please support these great schemes: visit www.spck.org.uk/support-us to find out more.